EinFach Englisch
Unterrichtsmodell

Series Editor: Hans Kröger

Gran Torino

edited by
Ulrike Klein
Gabriele Kugler-Euerle

Vorwort

Einzelarbeit

Partnerarbeit

Gruppen-
arbeit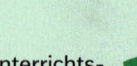

Unterrichts-
gespräch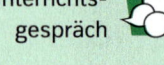

Schreib-
auftrag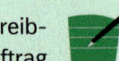

Hausaufgabe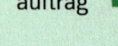

Audio-CD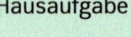

filmische
Präsentation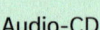

Projekt, offene
Aufgabe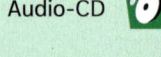

kreative
Aufgabe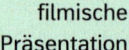

szenisches
Spiel,
Rollenspiel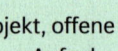

Der Titel der Reihe **EinFach Englisch** verdeutlicht Zielsetzung und Programm zugleich. Einerseits soll Schülerinnen und Schülern auf einfache Art und Weise der Zugang zu klassischen, aber auch neuen literarischen Werken und Filmen ermöglicht werden, andererseits sollen Lehrerinnen und Lehrern in der Praxis erprobte Unterrichtsmodelle angeboten werden, die die wichtigsten methodisch-didaktischen Ansätze ihres Faches Englisch abdecken. Dabei sind die Modelle direkt, ohne langes Einlesen einsetzbar und stellen Unterrichtsarbeit konkret vor. Als besonders hilfreich für die Praxis haben sich dabei folgende Aspekte erwiesen, die für die Gestaltung der Reihe wesentlich sind:

- Überblick über **Figurenkonstellation**, ggf. **Filmszenen** und **Inhalt**
- **Klausuren** mit **Erwartungshorizont**
- **Arbeitsblätter**, **Tafelbilder** und **Leitfragen** für den Unterricht
- **Piktogramme** als Hinweise auf **Unterrichts-** und **Arbeitsformen**

Das Prinzip der „**Components**" ermöglicht darüber hinaus den variablen Einsatz der Modelle in unterschiedlich konzipierten Unterrichtsreihen. Dabei stehen Machbarkeit und Praxisnähe stets im Vordergrund.

> Das vorliegende Modell bezieht sich auf die DVD *Gran Torino*. Warner Bros. Pictures, 2009.

Sprachliche Betreuung: Michelle R. Kloppenburg

© 2018 Bildungshaus Schulbuchverlage Westermann Schroedel Diesterweg Schöningh Winklers GmbH,
Georg-Westermann-Allee 66, 38104 Braunschweig
www.westermann.de

Druck A² / Jahr 2023
Alle Drucke der Serie A sind im Unterricht parallel verwendbar.

Umschlaggestaltung: Jennifer Kirchof
Druck und Bindung: Westermann Druck GmbH, Georg-Westermann-Allee 66, 38104 Braunschweig

ISBN 978-3-14-**041295**-7

Getting started

"Gran Torino"

Realign all the stars
Above my head
Warning signs
Travel far
I drink instead
On my own
Oh, how I've known
The battle scars
And worn out beds

Gentle now
A tender breeze blows
Whispers through a Gran
Torino
Whistling another tired song

Engines hum and bitter
dreams grow
Heart locked in a
Gran Torino
It beats a lonely rhythm all
night long

These streets are old
They shine with the things

I've known
And breaks through the trees
Their sparkling

Your world
Is nothing more
Than all
The tiny things
You've left behind

So tenderly
Your story is
Nothing more
Than what you see
Or
What you've done
Or will become
Standing strong
Do you belong
In your skin
Just wondering

May I be so bold and stay
I need someone to hold
That shudders my skin
Their sparkling

These are lines from the title song of the movie *Gran Torino* which allude to the movie's central themes and characters. What do you think?

- Is the movie about love, joy, pain, regret, bitterness, loneliness, death, violence, the past, the present?
- Is it the story of a man, a woman, two friends, a couple?
- Which words from the lyrics convey these ideas?

Zu den *Klausuren* und einigen *Copies* wurden Lösungen ergänzt – zu finden im Webshop unter „Lösungen" (Gratis-Download für Lehrerinnen und Lehrer).

Component 1: Presenting the film   25

The film

The making of *Gran Torino*

Clint Eastwood was 78 when he read popular TV actor Nick Schenk's first attempt at a screenplay. The script is based on the author's experience at a Minnesota Ford assembly plant where he was working side by side with several Korean War veterans who had come back from battle full of trauma and prejudice toward all Asians. Schenk's interests then focused further on the contradictive truths of the Hmong, a mountain-based migratory Chinese people, many of whom had come to Laos at the time of the Secret War, which started in 1965 and kept secret by the US government. The Hmong fought on the American side, but only some were allowed to come to the United States after the Americans left Vietnam in 1974. Many others ended up in Communist prison camps. Wherever they went they were met with suspicion, prejudice and rejection for something they did not have to answer for.

Throughout his work as a director, Eastwood has shown that his interest lies in translating emotionally resonant stories to the big screen. Consequently, he says he likes the dilemmas that the main character Walt Kowalski has to go through as well as Walt's obsoleteness in an antique America that may have become obsolete, too. In the following, read a short excerpt from an interview with Clint Eastwood:

Q: Why did you want to play Walt Kowalski?

Clint Eastwood: I liked the fact he was kind of crazy and an equal opportunity insulter, a unique character I thought I knew well. Growing up, I knew a lot of people like that. It seems in that era nobody was scared to say what they thought. This is a guy who is a Korean War veteran, whose wife just passed away at the beginning of the story. He's estranged from his two adult sons who he thinks have counted him out. His family doesn't care too much about him. They are grown up and don't want to hang out with an old guy. The grandkids don't want to hang out either, except if they might inherit something from him. Most of his friends have died. He has worked at the Ford Motor Company for 50 years and his neighborhood, which used to be all automobile people, has been taken over by immigrants. And he doesn't like the changes that he sees.

[...] Walt is an obsolete person. He's a little bit like Frankie Dunn, from *Million Dollar Baby*, and Sergeant Highway, from *Heartbreak Ridge*, those kind of guys who are out of synch with society and the modern world. He doesn't know how to relate to anybody. Nothing is the same and he's kind of cynical about it too. But he ends up learning tolerance with someone belonging to a country he's never even heard of.

"Clint Eastwood talks Gran Torino" by WalesOnline, 24 February 2009, updated 28 March 2013, https://www.walesonline.co.uk/lifestyle/showbiz/clint-eastwood-talks-gran-torino-2125543 [29.01.2018]

In 2008, Eastwood finished the shoot of his film in his standard thirty days and the movie went into release in January 2009. Although it received much acclaim from critics it was ignored in the Oscar nominations as "too negative and prejudicial".

In his 30th film as director, Clint Eastwood once again also takes on the leading role in which he portrays an aged and grieving Polish-American Korean War veteran who, having lost his wife, also seems to have lost his anchor in a world that has become alien. Suffering from an illness which is literally taking his breath away, estranged from his children and family, and left with only a handful of buddies to share a joke and beer with he has become cynical and withdrawn but still shows an enormous willpower and physical ability to fight on whenever the need arises. Bitter and prejudiced toward the Hmong in whom he sees the stereotypical reflection of the North Koreans he battled during the war, he doesn't spare them crude racist remarks after they have taken over and messed up his neighborhood. When he is accidentally drawn into their world and begins to open up to their culture he, however, must acknowledge their strong bond of common human experience, which explains his readiness to make the ultimate sacrifice and hunt down the enemy in defense of the people he understands are his friends.

The screen persona of the real-life loner struggling to find his way out of his emotional wilderness is a constant motive in the movies that the enduring Hollywood star Clint Eastwood has been acting in, directing or producing for more than fifty years. The actor has become the perfect impersonation of the aloof nihilist, estranged from a larger social order, resolute in his loneliness, the mysterious embittered man who needs nothing and no one beyond himself. The following quotations serve to illustrate this.

"Clint Eastwood is a tall, chiseled piece of lumber – a totem pole with feet … Eastwood seems to be chewing on bullet castings." (James Wolcott)

"People can know him for years and never be sure of what he's thinking. He's one of the warmest people in the world, but there's a certain distance, a certain mystery to him." (Sandra Locke)

"I'm an actor playing roles; all of them and none of them are me." (Clint Eastwood)

"After seventeen years of bouncing my head against the wall, hanging around sets, maybe influencing certain camera set-ups with my own opinions, watching actors go through all kinds of hell without any help, and working with both good directors and bad ones, I'm at the point where I'm ready to make my own pictures. I stored away all the mistakes I made and saved up all the good things I learned, and now I know enough to control my own projects and get what I want out of actors." (Clint Eastwood)

"We live in more of a pussy generation now, where everybody's become used to saying, 'Well, how do we handle it psychologically?' In (the old) days, you just punched the bully back and duked it out. Even if the guy was older and could push you around, at least you were respected for fighting back, and you'd be left alone from then on." (Clint Eastwood)

Although Eastwood insists that the movies he has been making are nothing but entertainment he is sending a strong message through most of them. His collective work proves a deep-rooted belief in "human nobility as the ultimate redemptive force" (Eliot, p. 7) of people living together, where connecting and bonding are essential.

Rather darkly and chillingly, *Gran Torino* also mirrors this in the way that here self-forgiveness and redemption mean self-sacrifice. There is no female romantic lead in this movie and no comic relief, the loner is the ultimate hero setting a young man's soul and future free through his gift of moral guidance and unselfish friendship.

American originals: Clint Eastwood and Walt Kowalski

Clint Eastwood: Facts and quotes

- life as "one big improvisation": Eastwood is known as actor, director, producer, musician (pianist), composer, businessmen, politician
- born in 1930, San Francisco, California
- raised in a working-class environment during the Great Depression
- drafted into the Army during the Korean War; remained at Ft. Ord, California as a swimming instructor
- has an estimated seven children with five women
- mayor of Carmel, a small community in California for two years
- registered Republican, then Libertarian because, as Eastwood puts it, "'I do believe if we just leave everybody alone, quit trying to think of ways to run everybody else's life, maybe we'd be better off. [...] It may be obsolete, that kind of thinking.'" ("'Eighty? It's just a number'" by Emma Brockes, guardian.com, 14 Feb 2009, https://www.theguardian.com/film/2009/feb/14/clint-eastwood-gran-torino [06.02.2018])
- icon of masculinity
- has been quoted multiple times as supporter of a stricter gun policy (gun control)
- famous roles as an actor: *Man with No Name* (in Sergio Leone's spaghetti Westerns), *Dirty Harry* (anti-hero cop Harry Callahan)
- as a director, Eastwood is known as a quiet authority, professional, very dedicated
- won National Board of Review award for Best Actor (*Gran Torino*, 2009): Eastwood wanted to play Walt from the beginning - "'[...] Walt may be obsolete. [...] But he does learn new things. [...] You take a guy who's way out opinionated, insulting to equal opportunity [...] [,] an insulter, and you put him with people where he's antagonistic as hell. And then all of a sudden he looks in the mirror and says, "I have more in common with these people than my own spoilt, rotten family."'" ("'Eighty? It's just a number'" by Emma Brockes, guardian.com, 14 Feb 2009, https://www.theguardian.com/film/2009/feb/14/clint-eastwood-gran-torino [06.02.2018])
- won Academy Awards for Best Director and Best Picture (*Unforgiven*, Western, 1992; *Million Dollar Baby*, sports drama, 2004)

Walt Kowalski: Quotes and (in)essentials

- the surname Kowalski is common in Poland; it translates into Smith
- the viewer gets to know Walt Kowalski as a Polish-American Korean War veteran, a retired Ford worker, a homophobe
- elderly retired Ford worker
- lives in Highland Park, Michigan, a rundown suburb of Detroit
- is a skillful and very masculine type: He believes that with "some WD-40, a vise grip, and a roll of duct tape [...] [a]ny man worth his salt can fix almost any problem [...]"
- loyal to his wife who died recently
- Walt is a veteran of the Korean War but he doesn't like to talk about his experiences, about killings and deaths
- owns a collection of weapons he used in the military; and he is not afraid to use them – as the viewer can tell from comments like this: "I'll blow a hole in your face then go inside and sleep like a baby."
- keeps the US Military's third highest award (a Silver Star) in his basement, but doesn't consider himself to be a hero
- has difficulty relating to his two grown-up sons: he doesn't understand how one of them sells Japanese cars while Walt worked in Ford for decades
- generally disapproves of the way the world is changing
- utters a total of 53 insults during the movie, most of them racial slurs
- his birthday horoscope gives a good hint as to what may happen ("'This year, you have to make a choice between two life paths. Second chances come your way. Extraordinary events culminate in what might seem to be an anti-climax.'") – and even though Walt believes it to be "a load of shit", he will sacrifice his life for the lives of the Asian family next door. His intentions are neatly summarized in Walt's line, "You've got your whole life ahead of you. But me, I finish things."

The plot – an overview

The linear structure of the movie follows a classic set-up in three acts with rising and falling tension.

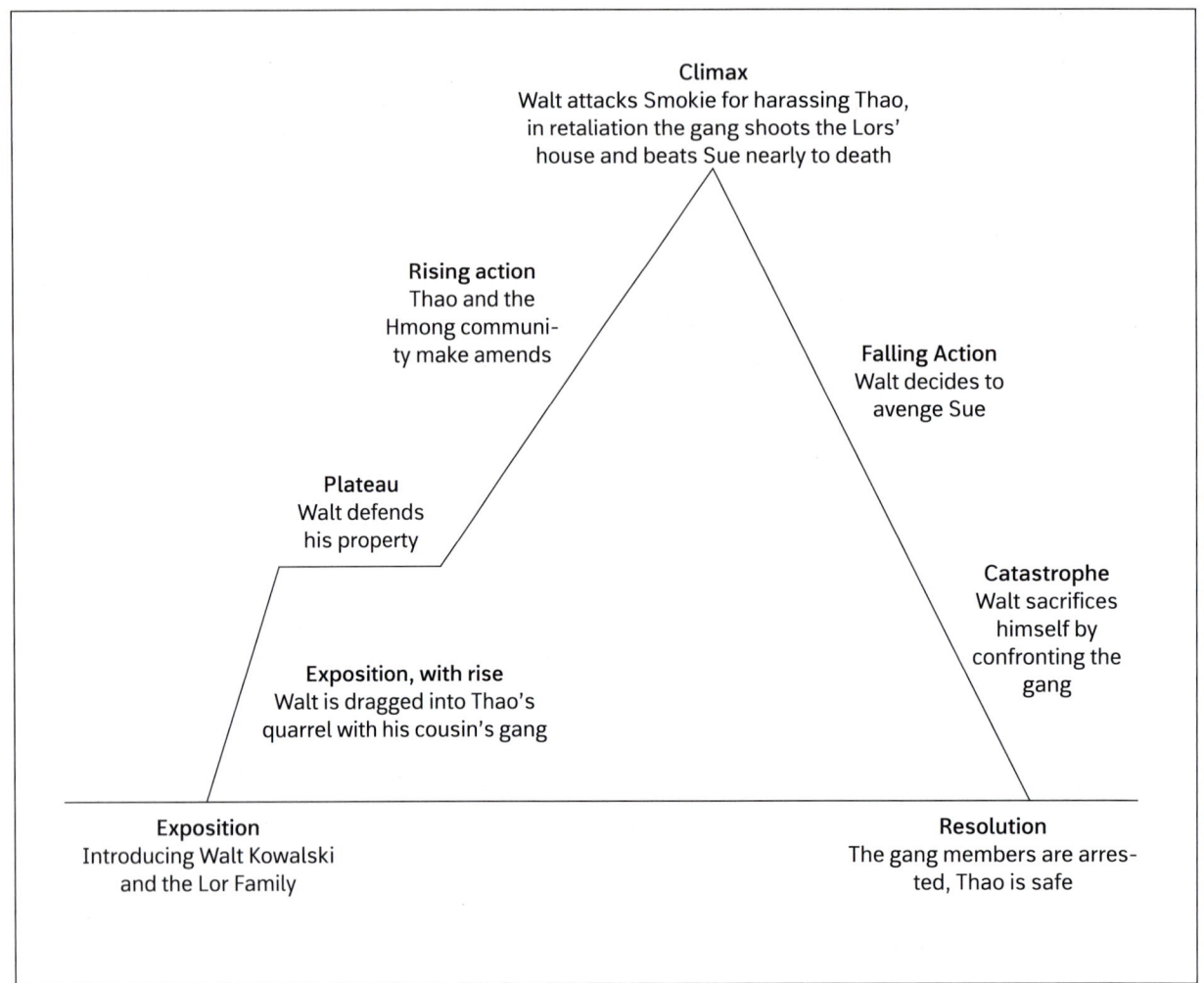

Climax
Walt attacks Smokie for harassing Thao, in retaliation the gang shoots the Lors' house and beats Sue nearly to death

Rising action
Thao and the Hmong community make amends

Falling Action
Walt decides to avenge Sue

Plateau
Walt defends his property

Catastrophe
Walt sacrifices himself by confronting the gang

Exposition, with rise
Walt is dragged into Thao's quarrel with his cousin's gang

Exposition
Introducing Walt Kowalski and the Lor Family

Resolution
The gang members are arrested, Thao is safe

Act One: About life and death

The set-up establishes the status quo of Walt Kowalski, the complex central character, full of flaws, who pursues a clear goal but is confronted with a conflict and predicament that is central to the story and provides tension. At the end of Act One, Walt is propelled into a new direction because backing out is no longer possible.

The opening of the film presents Walt Kowalski, a grim looking, stony-faced elderly man, during the funeral service for his wife. He shows open disdain for his unsympathetic family and the priest's eulogy. Later, Walt also keeps his distance from the mourners who mingle at his well-kept home in a suburban part of an industrial town. The Silver Star in the basement of his home establishes Walt's past as a Korean War Veteran. This may explain Walt's ensuing racist comments on Asian people streaming into the neighbouring rundown house – "Jesus Christ, how many swamp rats can they cram into a living room?" – and the way he fobs off his young neighbour's (Thao) polite request. Aloof and crabby, Walt also denies Father Janovich's offer of support and confession.

Meanwhile, the viewer is given a glimpse into the neighbouring house where Hmong are celebrating a new life and meets the other central character, Thao, an adolescent, uncomfortable in his role as the sole male member of an otherwise all-female household. He has difficult dealings with his cousin's gang who want to recruit him and force him to steal Walt's Ford Gran Torino in an initiation rite. Walt catches him in the act, but Thao can escape.

When a fight between the members of the Lor family next door and the Asian gang crosses the line from Thao's house and spills onto Walt's property, Walt intervenes by force of arms.

In these opening scenes, the film presents opposing settings: that of the American Walt Kowalski, a Korean War veteran and retired Ford autoworker, who has become misanthropic, withdrawn, alienated from his family, critical of the church, and a stranger in his own neighbourhood; and that of Thao and his Hmong family next door, still in touch with their cultural traditions and apart from American society, disconcerted by the American ways. Both are trapped in a hostile neighbourhood which has been on a constant decline, leaving it neglected and controlled by gangs.

Act Two: The hero of the neighbourhood

In this act the protagonist must react in new surroundings and figure out the way his neighbours live their lives. This section leads to the point of no return for Walt, who will become fully committed to saving Thao from suffering a major setback. The pace accelerates, the conflict is overwhelming: At the end of this act the protagonist is left with only one option: he must make one last, all-or-nothing effort.

Because Walt saved Thao from the gang, members of the Hmong community bring flowers and food to Walt's doorstep. At first irritated and angry, Walt accepts these offerings after Sue, Thao's sister, introduces him to the Hmong culture. In a rundown part of town he had rescued her from a dangerous situation with some black youths. Offended and disillusioned by his family on his birthday, Walt accepts Sue's invitation to a barbecue at their home. At first uncertain how to behave in these new and strange surroundings he soon enjoys the food and is left dumbfounded when the family shaman reads him and can precisely describe his state of mind. He painfully realizes that he actually feels closer to the people in this house, who can empathize more easily, than his "own spoiled-rotten family."

This also goes for Thao whose services Walt accepts as a way to make amends for the boy's attempt at stealing his Gran Torino. Under Walt's watchful eye, Thao does chores in the neighbourhood, gaining in skills and self-confidence. Slowly a friendship on equal terms can develop, which leads to Walt getting Thao a job on a construction site. Walt is certain that "Every tool has a purpose. Every thing has a job to do. They are all used, useful and necessary."

Walt's repeated coughing up of blood proves to be a serious illness during his visit to a doctor – a truth that he, however, cannot share with anyone.

When the gang attacks Thao and hurts him, Walt knocks down Smokie, the gang leader, in front of Thao's house. In retaliation the gang captures Sue, beats her up and rapes her.

Act Three: Redemption

The protagonist determines his own fate – Walt faces the hardest challenge of his life, which takes him and the plot to the ultimate showdown.

Thao wants to seek revenge for the attack on his sister and turns to Walt for help. Ignoring the priest's words of warning Walt carefully works out a plan which does not include Thao. This is how Walt justifies his decision to leave Thao out of it: "you wanna know what it's like to kill a man? Well, it's goddamn awful, that's what it is. The only thing worse is getting a medal... for killing some poor kid that wanted to just give up, that's all. Yeah, some scared little gook just like you. I shot him in the face with that rifle you were holding in there a while ago. Not a day goes by that I don't think about it, and you don't want that on your soul." After locking Thao up in the basement of his house, Walt confronts the gang at their house. Unarmed himself, he provokes them to kill him in order to save Thao and Sue from the clutches of the gang and give them peace. Walt leaves his Gran Torino to Thao and his house to the church, giving his own family a final brush-off for their insensitivity.

Scene Index

	Title	Location	In focus
Act One: About Life and Death			
00:00:50	1. The funeral service	church	Walt's face showing contempt for the disrespectful behaviour of his grandchildren and the priest's unconvincing eulogy
00:03:46	2. The post-service reception	Walt's house	Cantankerous Walt keeping his distance from family and friends
00:09:35	3. A celebration of life	the Lors' house	unfamiliar ceremonies and a happy gathering of friends and family
00:11:08	4. Two homes in perspective	Walt's house vs. the Lors' house	Walt's well-kept home, the Lors' dilapidated home
00:11:52	5. Father Janovich calls on Walt	Walt's porch	Walt's intransigence towards the priest's efforts
00:12:41	6. Thao and the Latino Gang	a wasted part of town	Thao's helplessness when confronted with the gang
00:15:10	7. Thao and his cousin's gang	in front of the Lor house	Thao giving into pressure
00:17:26	8. Hanging out with the guys	a veteran's bar	Walt giving into the priest's pleading for a conversation
00:20:05	9. The initiation rite	Walt's garage at night	Walt surprising Thao in his garage, a shot rings out
00:22:07	10. A father-son conversation	intercutting between Walt's garage and Mitch's house	the difficult relationship between Walt and his son
00:23:13	11. Back to normal	Walt's porch	Walt slurring the Asians in his neighbourhood
00:24:09	12. Get off my lawn	Walt's front yard	Walt ending the brawl between Spider's gang and the Lor family
Act Two: The Hero of the Neighbourhood			
00:26:43	13. Honouring Walt	Walt's porch	Walt's grumpy refusal of food and flowers that the Hmong bring to his doorstep
00:28:45	14. Persisting	Walt's porch	Walt repeating his refusal towards the priest to go to confession

	Title	Location	In focus
00:30:56	**15.** Chums	a barber shop	Walt and the barber bantering
00:31:28	**16.** Back off!	a rundown part of the neighbourhood	Walt backing Sue as she fends off a group of African-American youths
00:36:06	**17.** A lesson in Hmong	Walt's pick-up	Walt learns about the Hmong people
00:38:20	**18.** Look at that	Walt's porch	Walt observing Thao assisting a neighbour
00:40:11	**19.** Birthday presents for Walt	Walt's dining room	Walt's irritation at the insensitive choice of presents
00:42:12	**20.** A second birthday	the Lors' house	Walt experiences Hmong culture and is read by the family shaman
00:53:48	**21.** The need to make amends	Walt's lawn	Walt agrees to Thao working for him
00:56:02	**22.** Thao's first day	Walt's front yard	Walt makes Thao count the birds
00:56:38	**23.** Getting to work	the houses of the neighbourhood	Walt directs Thao's maintenance work on the neighbouring houses
00:59:59	**24.** Not a good time	Walt's bathroom and front door	Walt coughs up blood and sends Thao away on his last day of work
1:00:53	**25.** In another world	a doctor's practice	Walt as the only white American in the waiting room
1:00:58	**26.** The line has cut off	intercutting between Walt's garage and Mitch's house	Walt is unable to confide in Mitch about the grim results of the medical test
1:03:36	**27.** Watch it!	Walt's porch	Walt pointing a finger gun at Spider's gang driving by
1:04:08	**28.** Tools	the Lors' kitchen and Walt's garage	Walt equipping Thao with his first tools, Thao confessing about the initiation rite
1:09:36	**29.** A role model	Walt's backyard	Sue complimenting Walt for being a mentor to Thao
1:10:31	**30.** Plans for life	Walt's garden	Walt encouraging Thao to take on a job in construction
1:13:02	**31.** Manning Thao up	the barber shop	Walt and the barber initiating Thao into men's talk
1:16:18	**32.** The right words	a construction site	Thao getting the job

	Title	Location	In focus
1:18:42	**33.** Proper tools	a hardware shop in town	Walt and Thao shaking hands
1:59:56	**34.** What now?	a back alley	Thao attacked by Spider's gang while returning home from work
1:21:34	**35.** It is not your problem	same back alley	Walt learning about the gang's attack on Thao
1:22:52	**36.** Lay your hands off him	Spider's house	Walt taking revenge and beating up Smokie
1:24:40	**37.** Why not the Gran Torino	Walt's back porch	Walt offering Thao the Gran Torino for a night out with his girlfriend
1:26:08	**38.** No, no, no	the Lors' house	Walt coming to the aid of the Lor family after the gang's shots and seeing Sue return home battered and broken

Act Three: Redemption

	Title	Location	In focus
1:30:19	**39.** Nothing's fair	Walt's living room	Walt not answering the priest's question if he will retaliate
1:33:23	**40.** This is going to end	Walt's kitchen	Walt calming Thao who has come because he wants them to seek revenge
1:35:02	**41.** Preparations	Walt's place, barber shop, church	Walt preparing for the final confrontation and locking Thao in the basement
1:42:52	**42.** Leaving too soon	in front of Spider's house	the priest pleading with police officers to prolong their watch of the house
1:42:46	**43.** Finishing things	in front of Spider's house	Walt provoking the gang into shooting him
1:48:24	**44.** Another funeral service	the church	Sue and Thao listening to the priest's eulogy for Walt in traditional Hmong costumes
1:49:50	**45.** To my friend	a lawyer's office	Thao learns that Walt has left him the Gran Torino

The characters – a first analysis

Walt Kowalski

Walt Kowalski, a Korean War veteran and retired Ford autoworker, lives in a suburban part of Detroit. His well-maintained brownstone house still reminds of a booming time for the city which is long past. The shrinking industry, changing demographics and rising crime have changed the neighbourhood where gangs have now become commonplace and turned Walt into an embittered, angry old man. Now that his wife has died and he feels estranged from his sons and their families, he centres his life on the daily chores for his house and garden and sometimes enjoys a quiet moment on the front porch with his dog Daisy and a can of beer. Squinting and growling he watches the paint-peeled rundown houses left and right and their Asian inhabitants who constantly remind him of a past that he is trying so hard to forget. On top of that a young priest notoriously disturbs his peace and badgers him to confess his sins on behalf of his late wife. But Walt's interests lie elsewhere: an occasional beer with the guys at the veteran's bar, a visit at the barber for a quick banter with his friend Martin are more his idea of a face-to-face talk between men.

Walt's attempt to live the rest of his days quietly in his house, however, is undermined by Thao, the boy from next door who becomes entangled in the gang activities of his cousin. Step by step Walt is drawn into the life of the family from next door. Astute and quick on the uptake, Walt realizes that his Hmong neighbours are not an enemy but an ally in a confusingly changed world and so he becomes committed to defending their younger generation's future. As Thao's mentor he lets the boy learn his skills and he teaches him right from wrong. As Thao's protector he combats the gang, fiercely and uncompromisingly, until they retaliate. Walt believes he can free Thao and his sister from the cycle of violence while at the same time finally atone his past in a heroic act of self-sacrifice.

Father Janovich

- the priest in the neighbourhood
- dedicated to his flock, persistent
- works on Walt's conscience

Spider and Smokie

- Thao's cousin and the cousin's gangmate
- examples of what Thao's future might have looked like

Thao Vang Lor

Thao and Walt complement each other. Thao has the physical strength of youth, Walt the skills and experience of old age. Thao uses his brains; Walt is a man of action. Where Thao holds back and endures, Walt growls and lashes out. Once aligned, they will make a good team but their beginnings are rough.

Toad. Zipperhead. Egg roll. This is what Thao, good-natured but rather inept, hears from Walt and he does not contradict him. His self-esteem is low. Caught between his bossy sister Sue, who orders him to do the household chores actually reserved for women in his culture, and the demands of a nagging grandmother who wants him to be the man in the house, he has withdrawn and spends his days hanging about the wasteland around him. The family does not have the money for him to go to college and he does not have a clue of how and where to find a job. Then there is his cousin Spider and his cousin's gang. They are interested in him, have been where he is now, and are not to be messed with today. So Thao gives gang membership a try but fails. He is not tough enough or so he believes. In fact, to put an end to the bullying from his cousin it takes another kind of bully: Walt. Dumbstruck he watches the same man who he tried to steal from defend him. When his family wants him to make amends, Thao works his way into Walt's respect, stoically and resigned at first, then with growing enthusiasm when he realizes his potentials. And so does Walt. In his friendship with the old man, Thao regains his self-respect and learns how to assert himself in a world where only self-confidence and effectivity can open doors. Too young to fully understand how life runs, however, he is devastated to see himself suffer the consequences of his failure. Impetuously he seeks revenge but Walt prevents him from throwing his life away.

Sue

- Thao's older sister, chatty and articulate
- reflective and adaptable
- feels at home in both worlds: the Hmong culture and Walt's universe

Phong

- Thao's nagging grandmother
- in the true sense of the word: Walt's spitting image

Das Unterrichtsmodell

Vorüberlegungen zum Einsatz des Films im Unterricht

Clint Eastwoods *Gran Torino* ist ein Film über Menschen in einem Land, das, einst geboren aus einer großen Idee, sein Versprechen nicht halten konnte und jetzt marode daniederliegt. Zumindest spiegelt dies der Mikrokosmos wieder, in dem Walt Kowalski und seine asiatischen Nachbarn um eine Zukunft in Würde ringen. Sie sind gestrandet in der Vorstadt, die ihnen beiden Heimat ist, die sie aber zunächst nicht miteinander teilen wollen. Der selbstgerechte, feindselige Walt glaubt in den Einwanderern den Grund zu sehen, warum er seine Welt, für die er gekämpft und gearbeitet hat, in ihrer Verwahrlosung nicht mehr wiedererkennen kann. Die scheuen, zuvorkommenden Einwanderer aus Fernost scheinen zufrieden unter ihresgleichen zu leben und sehen in ihm den eigentlichen Eindringling. Ihre Leben vernetzen sich plötzlich auf eigenartige Weise. Gewalt bringt sie zusammen, und aus dieser Erfahrung erwachsen neue Bindungen. Das Gefühl von Zugehörigkeit und innerer Verbundenheit schöpft sich nicht länger mehr allein aus traditionellen Konzepten. Die Kultur, aus der man stammt, die Generation, der man angehört, die Familie, die einen umgibt, all diese Kategorien werden überlagert von der Orientierung an gemeinsamen Werten, die allumfassend scheinen. Richtig und falsch werden gemeinsam neu ausgedeutet, Mut und Verantwortung, Mitgefühl und Hingabe, Selbstachtung und Respekt helfen neue Wege zu gehen.
Seinen Platz im Leben zu finden, Bindungen zu prüfen und neu zu verknüpfen, Zugehörigkeit als ambivalent zu verstehen und dennoch nach ihr zu streben, davon spricht der Film somit auch.
Dies sind auch die Themen, die im Leben der Schülerinnen und Schüler von Bedeutung sind. In der genauen Beobachtung der Figuren können sie sich kritisch mit den Antworten, die der Film auf Fragen der Identität und des Zusammenlebens gibt, auseinandersetzen.

Aspekte der Filmarbeit im Unterricht

Das Unterrichtsmodell wurde für die Filmarbeit in der Kursstufe erarbeitet. Es priorisiert die inhaltliche Auseinandersetzung mit Figuren und Themen und bindet filmanalytische Aufgaben an geeigneter Stelle funktional mit ein. Deshalb wurde an dieser Stelle auf eine ausführliche Darstellung von filmischen Gestaltungsmitteln verzichtet. *Copy 0* bietet lediglich einen knappen aber hoffentlich hilfreichen Überblick.
In der Erfahrung der Autorinnen hat es sich bewährt, dass während der Unterrichtseinheit die Schülerinnen und Schüler selbständig mit dem Film arbeiten können. Die Nutzung mobiler Endgeräte wie Handy oder Tablets ermöglicht über *Streaming*-Verfahren einen flexiblen Umgang mit den Szenen des Films, so dass sowohl zu Hause als auch im Unterricht individuelle Sehgewohnheiten, Interessen und Arbeitstempi berücksichtigt werden können.

Konzeption des Unterrichtsmodells

Zielsetzungen der Arbeit mit *Gran Torino*

Die Arbeit an Clint Eastwoods *Gran Torino* ist so konzipiert, dass die Schülerinnen und Schüler als souveränes Kinopublikum angesprochen werden. Deshalb empfiehlt es sich aus unserer Sicht auch, den Film zunächst im Ganzen zu sehen, erste Reaktionen einzufangen und für die produktive Weiterarbeit zu nutzen. Des Weiteren ist es sinnvoll, Schwerpunkte der Arbeit am

Film mit den Schülerinnen und Schülern abzustimmen. Die Organisation und Struktur dieses Unterrichtsmodells möchte Ihnen deshalb möglichst hohe Flexibilität gewährleisten.

Component 1 umfasst aus diesem Grund lediglich *Copies* mit einer Vielzahl von Aufgaben, die das Hör-Sehverstehen der Schülerinnen und Schüler fördern, das Globalverstehen des Films und das Detailverstehen wichtiger Szenen sichern und so die vertiefende Analyse vorbereiten. Mit den Materialien dieses *Components* können Sie gegebenenfalls auch Ihre eigene individuelle Unterrichtsplanung erarbeiten und auch eine Filmpräsentation in Abschnitten begleiten. Die drei folgenden *Components* zeigen exemplarisch, wie die Inhalte, Figuren und Themen des Films behandelt werden können und wie Global- und Detailverstehen in ein Unterrichtsszenarium eingebunden werden können.

Die inhaltlichen Zielsetzungen dieser drei Components ergeben sich aus der obigen Analyse des Themenspektrums. Im Zentrum von *Component 2* und *Component 3* stehen die beiden Hauptfiguren des Films: Walt Kowalski und Thao Vang Lor. In jeweils drei Schritten begleiten die gewählten Fragestellungen und Aufgaben die Entwicklung dieser beiden Figuren und ihre Suche nach Zugehörigkeit. Persönlich-individuelle Aspekte werden im Prozess dabei zunehmend gesellschaftlich relevant ausgedeutet, so dass in *Component 4* die sozialkritischen Aspekte des Films aufgedeckt und bearbeitet werden können.

Das Medium Film wird in allen *Components* dieser Unterrichtspraxis als Kommunikationsanlass genutzt. Hierbei stehen konsequenterweise Analyseaufgaben im Zentrum der Unterrichtsarbeit, die individuelle Verstehensprozesse und eigenständige Bewertungen fordern und fördern. Dabei ist es wichtig, dass im Bereich der Unterrichtskommunikation funktional vorgegangen wird. Arbeitsprozesse sind kooperativ angelegt, das Grundprinzip des *Think-Pair-Share* sichert hier die konsequente Aktivierung aller Schülerinnen und Schüler und fördert somit die authentische fremdsprachliche Kommunikation. Das Plenum oder Unterrichtsgespräch dient der Strukturierung der Arbeitsprozesse und Sicherung der Ergebnisse. Umfangreichere Schreibproduktionen schließen die jeweiligen Unterrichtsschritte ab und bieten somit in Verbindung mit den Verstehensaufgaben eine nachhaltige Vorbereitung der Klausur.

Klausur

Connie Cass, Jennifer Agiesta, Dennis Junius: It's not cool to use slurs online, even if you're 'jk'

In a shift in attitude, most young people now say it's wrong to use racist or sexist slurs online, even if you're just kidding. But when they see them, they don't take much personal of-
5 fense.

A majority of teens and young adults who use the Internet say they at least sometimes see derogatory words and images targeting various groups. They often dismiss that stuff as just
10 joking around, not meant to be hurtful, according to a new poll from The Associated Press-NORC Center for Public Affairs Research and MTV.

Americans aged 14 to 24 say people who are
15 overweight are the most frequent target, followed by gay people. Next in line for online abuse: blacks and women.

"I see things like that all the time," says Vito Calli, 15, of Reading, Pa. "It doesn't really both-
20 er me unless they're meaning it to offend me personally." Even then he tries to brush it off. Calli, whose family emigrated from Argentina, says people tease him online with jokes about Hispanics, but "you can't let those things get to
25 you."

He's typical of many young people surveyed. The majority say they aren't very offended by slurs in social media or cellphone text messages – even such inflammatory terms as
30 "bitch" or "fag" or the N-word. Yet like Calli, most think using language that insults a group of people is wrong. The high school sophomore says he has tried, with difficulty, to break his habit of calling anything uncool "gay" or
35 "retarded."

Compared with an AP-MTV poll two years ago, young people today are more disapproving of using slurs online. Nearly 6 in 10 say using discriminatory words or images isn't all
40 right, even as a joke. Only about half were so disapproving in 2011. Now, a bare majority say it's wrong to use slurs even among friends who know you don't mean it. In the previous poll, most young people said that was OK.

But the share who come across slurs online has 45 held steady. More than half of young users of YouTube, Facebook and gaming communities such as Xbox Live and Steam say they sometimes or often encounter biased messages on those platforms. 50
Why do people post or text that stuff? To be funny, according to most young people who see it. Another big reason: to be cool. Less than a third said a major reason people use slurs is because they actually harbor hateful 55 feelings toward the groups they are maligning.

"Most of the time they're just joking around, or talking about a celebrity," Jeff Hitchins, a white 24-year-old in Springfield, Pa., said 60 about the insulting references to blacks, women and gays that he encounters on the Vine and Instagram image-sharing sites. "Hate speech is becoming so commonplace, you forget where the words are coming from, and 65 they actually hurt people without even realizing it."

Some slurs are taken more seriously than others. Racial insults are not that likely to be seen as hurtful, yet a strong majority of those sur- 70 veyed – 6 in 10 – felt comments and images targeting transgender people or Muslims are. Almost as likely to be viewed as mean-spirited are slurs against gays, lesbians and bisexual people, and those aimed at people who are 75 overweight [...].

Erick Fernandez of West New York, N.J., says what people share online reflects the influence of song lyrics and music videos and movies. Fernandez, 22, said he was "probably very 80 loose" about that himself before he was chosen for a diversity summer camp in high school that explained why phrases like "That's so gay" are hurtful. Now a college student, he routinely sees insulting language for women 85 and people of color bandied about online. "I try to call some of my friends out on it but it's really to no avail," Fernandez said. "They brush it

off and five minutes later something else will come
90 out. Why even bother?"

In the poll, young people said they were less likely to ask someone to stop using hurtful language on a social networking site than face to face.

Alexandria Washington said she's accustomed to see-
95 ing men who wouldn't say offensive things to her in person post pictures of "half-naked women in sexual positions," followed by demeaning comments and slurs like "whore" and "ratchet." "They'll post anything online, but in person it's a whole different sto-
100 ry," said Washington, 22, a graduate student in Tallahassee, Fla.

There seems to be a desensitizing effect. Those who report more exposure to discriminatory images and words online are less likely to say it's wrong than
105 those who rarely or never encounter it. Context is crucial, too. Demeaned groups sometimes reclaim slurs as a way of stripping the words of their power – like the feminist "Bitch" magazine or gay rights activists chanting "We're here, we're queer, get used to
110 it!"

Washington, who is African-American, said that on most days she doesn't come across racial slurs on social media. But she stumbles upon bigoted words when race is in the news, such as surrounding President Barack Obama's re-election, and finds them 115 hurtful in that serious context.

Likewise, Calli, the high school student originally from Argentina, said he could stomach almost any name-calling but gets upset when someone uses a falsehood to denigrate immigrants. 120

Jeffrey Bakken, 23, a producer at a video game company in Chicago, said the bad stuff online, especially slurs posted anonymously, shouldn't overshadow what he sees as the younger generation's stronger commitment to equal rights for minorities and gays 125 than its elders.

"Kids were horrible before the Internet existed," Bakken said. "It's just that now it's more accessible to the public eye."

(944 words)

from PBS Newshour, 20 November 2013, http://www.pbs.org/newshour/rundown/its-not-cool-to-use-slurs-online-even-if-youre-jk/[29.01.2018]. Copyrighted 2013 Associated Press. 256638:0118PF

Assignments

1. Tick the correct statement(s) or complete the sentence as indicated in the assignment. Give a quote from the text to support the correct statement: Write the line number(s) plus the first three and the last three words of the quote. (Comprehension)

1. Tick the correct statement. (1 credit)
   When it comes to racial slurs online the author of the text believes young people's reaction is
   ☐ contradictory.
   ☐ divided.
   ☐ resolute.
   ☐ convincing.

   line(s): _____   quote: _____

   _____

2. Tick the correct statement. (1 credit)
   Data from the survey confirms that adolescents in general
   ☐ put aside online discrimination of people.
   ☐ find online discrimination a laughing matter.
   ☐ follow online discrimination of people on a daily basis.
   ☐ ignore online discrimination of people.

   line(s): _____   quote: _____

   _____

© Westermann Gruppe
Best.-Nr. 041295

3. Tick whether the statement is true or false.   (1 credit)
   Vito Calli's words illustrate a recent trend in young
   people's handling of online slurs.   ☐ true   ☐ false

   line(s): _____   quote: _____

   _____

4. Complete the sentence.   (2 credits)
   The 2013 survey shows a change in attitude compared to 2011 because

   beforehand _____

   and now _____

   line(s): _____   quote: _____

   line(s): _____   quote: _____

   _____

5. Tick the correct statement.   (1 credit)
   People who post slurs online usually expose
   ☐ racist mindsets.
   ☐ carelessness.
   ☐ humour.
   ☐ deliberation.

6. Tick whether the statement is true or false.   (1 credit)
   Data shows that people are more sensitive about slurs
   concerning ethnicity than any other topic.   ☐ true   ☐ false

   line(s): _____   quote: _____

   _____

7. Tick the correct statements.   (3 credits)
   ☐ Online defamation and overt discriminating behaviour do not necessarily go together.
   ☐ Personal experience of discrimination makes people more sensitive.
   ☐ People feel encouraged by the media to post slurs online.
   ☐ Without the Internet, the problem of people using slurs would not exist.
   ☐ Young people increasingly report online slurs to the social networks.

   line(s): _____   quote: _____

   _____

2. Read the following quote by Yehuda Berg:

content: 10 VP
language: 15 VP

"Words have energy and power with the ability to help, to heal,
to hinder, to hurt, to harm, to humiliate, and to humble."

Compare the text and the movie on this issue. (Analysis)

3. Choose **ONE** of the following:

content: 10 VP
language: 15 VP

a) Family, race, neighbourhood: Which of these three promotes the
greatest sense of belonging?
Illustrate your view with examples from the movie *Gran Torino*. (Composition)

b) "I am no hero." (Walt Kowalski)
Discuss this quote from the movie (Composition).

© Westermann Gruppe
Best.-Nr. 041295

Kommunikationsprüfung

Monologue Partner A: Defining moments

- Reacting to the text below compare the experience of this woman to Thao's experience in the movie *Gran Torino* and explain how important such 'defining moments' are in the life of a person.
- What and who else can help to promote the integration of people coming from foreign cultures? Justify your answer.

Growing up in Banning, Calif., Vang was [...] in classes with Hmong- and Mexican-American students. When fifth grade began, however, she found herself in a class dominated by white children [...]. Still, she was quiet, until the day her teacher noticed her on the playground.
"You know, Be Vang, you have this thing about you," she remembers him telling her. "You're loud,
5 you're strong, you command these little Hmong boys to do things. That's what I need in the classroom. You are going to speak up. I am going to hear your voice."
Had that not happened, she said, she wonders where she might be today.
Be Vang, currently principal at Mississippi Creative Arts School and a member of the Hmong community in St. Paul.

from: Anthony Lonetree, "St. Paul educator on the move integrates Hmong-American experience into schools," StarTribune, 9 June 2014, http://www.startribune.com/st-paul-educator-integrates-hmong-american-experience-into-schools/262466411/ [18.12.2017]

Monologue Partner B: Defining moments

- Reacting to the text below compare the experience of this woman to Thao's experience in the movie *Gran Torino* and explain what effective 'sponsorship or mentorship' is like.
- What if people from foreign cultures are not able to experience such 'defining moments' when they are new to a country? Justify your answer.

In Laos, we raised our own chickens and did everything with them until they were on the table to eat. In the dormitory of the home for asylum-seekers, they gave us these chickens with the feathers off in shiny wrappers. We understood that they were "ready to cook." I was making dinner for our group when our sponsor stopped by for a visit. She laughed when she saw the chicken in the
5 boiling water and told me I had to take the shiny wrapper off first. She also told us we didn't need to douse the stove with water to put out the heat. The next meal, the sponsor came by and cooked with us. I taught her how to make Hmong food and she taught me how to use the German ingredients and appliances to prepare it.

from: *Belonging: The Social Dynamics of Fitting In as Experienced by Hmong Refugees in Germany and Texas* by Faith Nibbs. Durham, North Carolina: Carolina Academic Press, 2014.

Dialogue: Basic human needs

This pyramid shows which needs must be fulfilled so that a person can reach self-actualization in life

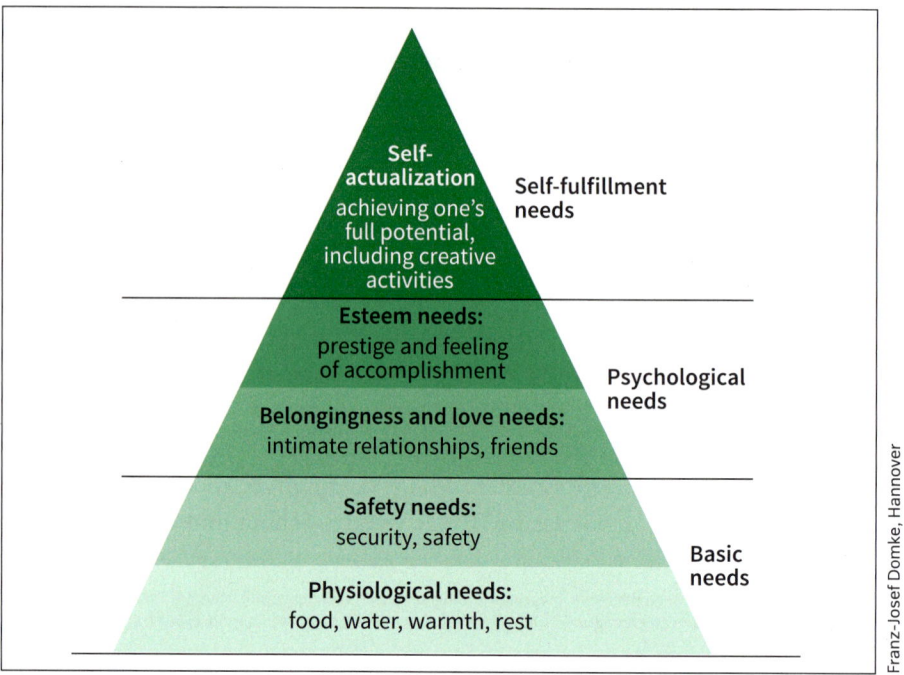

Franz-Josef Domke, Hannover

- Take turns in explaining who or what can support young people like Thao Vang Lor on their way to self-actualization.
  Does the responsibility in each stage lie solely with the persons themselves?
  What can their families and their private environment, institutions, society, the government contribute?
- Discuss and agree whether this illustration represents Thao and his situation at the end of the movie.

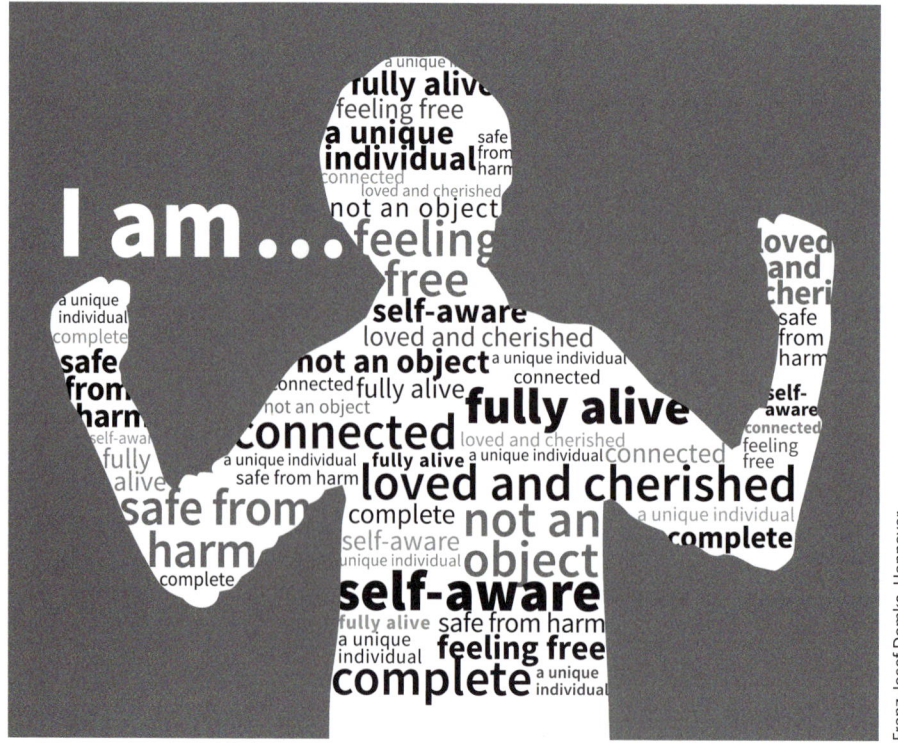

Franz-Josef Domke, Hannover

Presenting the film

Die in diesem *Component* zusammengestellten *Copies* beinhalten Aufgabenstellungen zum Globalverstehen und Detailverstehen. Letzteres wird immer durch eine Kontextualisierung der Szene(n) eingeleitet und fokussiert dann auf die Figuren und Themen des Filmes. Die Analyse filmischer Mittel ist eher zurückhaltend und immer nur funktional eingearbeitet, um der thematischen Arbeit mehr Raum zu geben.

Gran Torino erzählt das Geschehen linear. Auch wenn er dies nicht in Echtzeit tut, so hat der Zuschauer dennoch den Eindruck, die Figuren durch die Ereignisse weniger aufeinanderfolgender Tage zu begleiten. Man arbeitet sich langsam vor und in die Figuren hinein, im Bemühen ihre Worte und ihr Handeln im nächsten Moment besser verstehen zu können. Um diese Absicht von Drehbuch und Regie auch im Klassenzimmer umzusetzen und dem Filmansatz so gerecht zu werden, plädieren wir für eine Gesamtpräsentation des Filmes vorab und nicht für ein episodisches Vorgehen. Dennoch können Sie sich im Falle einer alternativen Herangehensweise auch effektiv an den Aufgabenapparaten auf den *Copies* in **Component 1** bedienen.

Die vier Aufgaben zum Globalverstehen (*Copies 1–5*) nutzen analytische und kreative Ansätze. So kann differenziert auf Vorlieben und Stärken in der Lerngruppe reagiert werden. Bewusst sind die Aufgaben nicht kleinschrittig entwickelt, sondern sollen es den Schülerinnen und Schülern ermöglichen, nach dem Ansehen des Films ihre individuellen Eindrücke mit anderen auszutauschen und erste Ergebnisse ihrer Beobachtungen nachhaltig zu sichern.

Die Aufgaben zum Detailverstehen werden in den **Components 2, 3** und **4** thematisch eingebettet, stehen aber mit den auf ihnen notierten Arbeitsaufträgen auch für sich. Alle diese Aufgaben führen immer wieder auf Szenen im Film zurück, die in der Rückschau der Ereignisse häufig zusätzliche Bedeutung erfahren. Anmerkung: Aus lizenzrechtlichen Gründen musste an einigen Stellen auf den Abdruck von Standbildern und Drehbuchauszügen verzichtet werden. Präzise Angaben, wo die Szene im Film zu finden ist, helfen aber die Fragen immer wieder am Film zu illustrieren.

In den **Components 2, 3** und **4** finden sich auf den *Copies* darüber hinaus Zusatztexte, die die Themen auch aus anderen Perspektiven beleuchten oder Hintergrundinformationen bieten.

Die Klausur sowie die Aufgabe für die Kommunikationsprüfung sind nach baden-württembergischem Muster erstellt, da der Film dort ein Teil des Schwerpunktthemas im Abitur ist *(the Ambiguity of Belonging)*.

The language of film

ambiance	The overall mood of a scene or setting	
antagonist	The main character in conflict with the film's hero(ine), lead character or protagonist (also: bad guy, or villain)	
camera angles	camera	purpose/effect
• bird's-eye view • high angle/crane • overhead shot 	positioned above	With high angle shots, the viewer looks down on the action. This makes people and objects appear smaller, less important, or even Insignificant, or helps to put them into a larger context.
• low angle/below shot	positioned below	Low angles may make characters look dominant, aggressive, and threatening. It focussed on the action, they will most often create an intimidating atmosphere.
• eye-level/straight-on angle	positioned at eye-level with the viewer or one of the characters involved	Eye-level shots are the most, common camera angle as they help to make the viewers feel port of the scene, as if they were confronting the person or object directly. This also makes the scene feel more 'realistic'.
• establishing shot (long or wide shot)	positioned at a distance or zoomed out so that particular objects, the location in general or characters appear relatively small in the frame	Establishing shots usually occur at the beginning of a scene (or a sequence) and help the viewer to identify the location and approximate time of the scene as a form of orientation.
• medium shot (one-/two-/three-shot 	positioned: at or zoomed to a medium distance so as to show a human figure from the waist or knees up, depending on the number of people or objects in the frame	Medium shots place the focus on the action/interaction of the people in the frame.
• close-up (CU) • extreme close-up (ECU) 	positioned or zoomed in to a close distance so that objects and people or certain aspects of them appear relatively large and fill the entire frame	CUs and ECUs focus attention on something and emphasize its importance; when facial expressions are in focus rather than the external action, it often makes us feel either more comfortable or extremely uncomfortable.
• insert(ed) CU	refers to a shot taken of a static object, which fills most of the frame and is inserted late during the editing process, typically between two shots of a character looking offscreen	inserted CUs are employed to emphasize a relevant object which could easily be overlooked in the complex mise en scène of the shot and/or to show what a character is looking at.

Illustrationen: Reinhild Kassing, Kassel

© Westermann Gruppe
Best.-Nr. 041295

• point of view shot (POV)	positioned so as to take the shot from the subjective perspective of one of the characters and usually coupled with a reaction shot	POYs are meant to show the audience the scene as if through the eyes of one of the characters.
• reaction shot	refers to a quick shot that records a character's or group's response to another character or some on-screen action or event	Reaction shots help viewers to feel more involved in the dialogue or the action.
• over-(the)-shoulder shot (OTS)	refers to a shot which records the action from behind he shoulder and/or head of one of the characters, who is usually looking in the direction of another character	OTSs help to link the characters involved in a scene by establishing their respective positions. By giving the viewers the impression that they are looking at a person or a group of people from the other person's point of view, OTSs help viewers to feel like they are actually interacting with the other character(s) in the film.
• reverse angle shot/ reverse shot	refers to a shot photographed from the opposite side of person/object to provide a different perspective	Reverse angle shots are typically used for scenes In which the focus Is on the dialogue and character interaction.

camera movement

• pan(ning)/tracking shot	camera movement from left to right (or vice versa), with the camera moving on a 'doily' (a platform on wheels)	Panning/tracking shots are used to follow the action -or to survey the overall setting. This gives viewers the feeling that they are part of the scene because they are following the action closely at eye-level.
• tilt (up or down)	camera movement upwards or downwards	A tilt can be used to emphasize the height of something, to simulate someone looking up or down or to surprise the viewers by focusing on a change.
• zoom in/out	refers to changing the framing of a shot from *wide angle* to *close-up* and vice versa	Zooming in serves to isolate a person or object from the surrounding environment and to put it into focus; zooming out is used to place something or someone within a larger context.

camera speed

• slow motion	a technique which makes people or objects appear to be moving more slowly than normal	Slow motion in films usually builds suspense, intensifies emotions or simply highlights the importance of the moment.
• fast motion	a technique which makes people or objects appear to be moving more quickly than normal	Fast motion usually creates a comic arid/or hectic effect.
• freeze frame	a frame image created by stopping the film in the middle of the action	Freeze frames are often used at the end of a film to indicate death, to introduce ambiguity, and to provide an iconic, lasting image.
cast	all of the actors appearing in a film	

Illustrationen: Reinhild Kassing, Kassel

credits	list of cast, crew, and other people involved in making a film (*opening credits* appear at the beginning, *closing credits* at the end)	
crew	all those involved in the technical production of a film, who are not actual performers	
critic	a person who publishes a review of a film, considering it from either an artistic or entertainment point of view	
cut	an essential part of the editing process; an abrupt change in camera angle, location or time, from one shot to another	
● cross-cutting	editing technique that combines two scenes or events by alternating between them or interweaving them with one another	Cross-cutting enables viewers to realize that the two actions are somehow linked, and the characters from the different lines of action are connected in some way.
● dissolve, burn-in/-out fade-in/-out	the visible image of one shot or scene is gradually replaced, super imposed or blended in or out (by an overlapping fade-out or fade-in and following dissolve) of the image from another shot or scene	This superimposition of shots is often used to suggest the passage of time or to, imitate hallucinatory states.
● match cut	a cut between two shots (outgoing and incoming), which are felt to be "matched" because they contain similar elements	A match cut emphasizes the continuity of the action and helps to link one scene to another more smoothly.
director	a director usually has the complete artistic control over all aspects of the film, such as casting, script editing, shot selection, shot composition, and editing, etc. On the film set, the director is also responsible for communicating to actors how a particular scene is to be performed.	
editing	the process by which the many separate camera takes of the filming process are selected, assembled, arranged, trimmed, structured, and spliced (= joined) together to form a complete sequence in line with the script	
eyeline	the direction in which a character is looking	Eyelines are often a way of letting the viewers know what (or whom) a character is Interested in.
focus	refers to the degree of sharpness and clarity in a film image; "out-of-focus": images are blurred and lack clear linear definition	
foreshadowing	refers to hints provided within a film (In the form of symbols, images, motifs, repetition, dialogue or mood) about the outcome of the plot, or about an upcoming action that will take place	This is often done in order to prepare viewers for later events, revelations, or plot developments; ominous music also often foreshadows danger or builds suspense.
frame	a single image of a film	
interior/exterior	a scene apparently shot indoors or out of doors	
lighting	refers to the overall illumination of the set and may be described in terms of the direction from which the light enters the set (front-lighting, back-lighting, side-lighting, top-lighting, cross-lighting) or simply in terms of the contrast between light and dark (high-key, low-key lighting)	
mise en scène	refers to all the elements within the frame of the film and how they are arranged In front of the camera includes, for example, the setting, overall decor, props, actors, costumes, makeup, lighting, performances and characters	
pace	the speed/tempo of the dramatic action, which is usually enhanced by the soundtrack and the speed of the dialogue, the type of editing, etc.	

© Westermann Gruppe
Best.-Nr. 041295

plot/plot point	refers to a series of dramatic events or actions that make up a film's narrative; a plot point is a key turning point or moment in a film's story that significantly advances the action; plot points either move the story forward or disrupt and complicate the plot
producer	a producer is responsible for raising funding, hiring personnel, and arranging the sale of a film to cinemas or the distribution rights for DVDs
props (abbreviation for properties)	refers to hand-held objects, decorations, or any other moveable items that actors use or interact with in a scene
protagonist	the lead or main character in a film; also known as the hero/heroine; contrast to antagonist
ratings	also known as the MPAA (Motion Picture Association of America) film rating system, first officially instituted in late 1968; it refers to the ever-evolving classification system for films, usually based upon age-appropriateness, and the judgment of a film's suitability for various audiences in terms of sexual content, offensiveness, or violence
release	refers to the first distribution and general public exhibition of a film to theatre audiences
running time	a measure of the duration or length of a film, usually about two hours for a feature film
script/screenplay	text written to be turned into a film that contains dialogue, as well as first ideas on staging like mise en scene, camera movement, etc.
set	in contrast to location, set refers to an artificially constructed environment used for filming.
shot	refers to a single image, the smallest compositional unit of a film's structure

sound	speech (dialogue) music noises (sound effects)	The sound in a fibs serves to • simulate reality, • create illusion generate the mood Musk, in particular, can help to • underline a character's emotions • evoke nostalgic feelings • foreshadow an event • build suspense • establish transitions between scenes • provide the viewer with a tone or an emotional attitude toward the story and/or the characters
tagline	very short summary of a film plot	
voice-over	commentary by an unseen narrator, an oft-screen voice or a character whose lips are not moving	The commentary helps to set the theme and often encourages the viewer to look for a deeper meaning in the action on the screen.

texts from: *EinFach Englisch: LA Crash ... verstehen.* Ed. by Ulrike Klein and Gabriele Kugler-Euerle. Paderborn: Schöningh 2014, S. 97–104.

For even more terms, go to: www.imdb.com/glossary/

The story of a summer

1. Put the screen shots in the chronological order of the film and add a title for each.
2. Work in pairs. One of you tells the story from Walt's, the other from Thao's view.
   Which situations and people alluded to in the screen shots would either talk about?

 A

 B

 C

D

 E

F

photos: *Gran Torino*, directed by Clint Eastwood, released 2009 by Warner Bros. Entertainment Inc.

actors (left to right): picture A: Sonny Vue, Bee Vang (Thao), Lee Mong Vang, Jerry Lee, Elvis Thao; B: Bee Vang; C: Doua Moua, Bee Vang; D: Bee Vang, Clint Eastwood; E: Ahney Her (Sue), Clint Eastwood; F: Dreama Walker (Ashley)

© Westermann Gruppe
Best.-Nr. 041295

(G)

(H)

(I)

(J)

(K)

(L)

(M)

photos: *Gran Torino*, directed by Clint Eastwood, released 2009 by Warner Bros. Entertainment Inc.

actors (left to right): G: Bee Vang; H: Christoper Carley, Clint Eastwood; I: Clint Eastwood; J: Bee Vang, John Caroll Lynch, Clint Eastwood; K: Bee Vang; L: Brooke Chia Thao, Choua Kue, Bee Vang, Clint Eastwood, Ahney Her; M: Bee Vang

31

Killed in a hail of bullets

Walt Kowalski is dead. The police investigate. They interview Thao, Sue and Father Janovich to learn more about the victim and the perpetrators.

1. List 10 questions they might ask.
2. In groups of three come up with the answers Walt's friends may have for them.
3. Enter the information into the police report.

	Case 01-78-090045	Location type		
INCIDENT	Offense: ☐ assault ☐ homicide ☐ other Weapon: Situation on arrival:			# of people arrested:
PERSON TYPES	Person type VICTIM	Name	Race	Sex
	Age: Occupation:			Fatal injuries:
	Person type SUSPECT	Name	Race	Sex
	Age: Occupation:			Relation to victim: Possible motive:
	Witness report on the incident:			

Thumbs up, thumbs down

beermedia – Fotolia.com

In blogs people often share their experience of something special.

1. Use this template for a spontaneous review of the film you have just seen.

Film blog: A review
Review of the film: _____
By: _____
My review:

2. Get together in groups of five or six and share your experience like in an online blog. Discuss your reactions and agree on five notions you will put in a proper review of the film after our analysis.

The plot of *Gran Torino*

The film's structure is linear. The viewer follows the chronology of the days that lead up to the final climax and the viewer can live through the emotions of the characters in the film. Formally, the film follows a classic set-up in three acts with rising and falling tension.

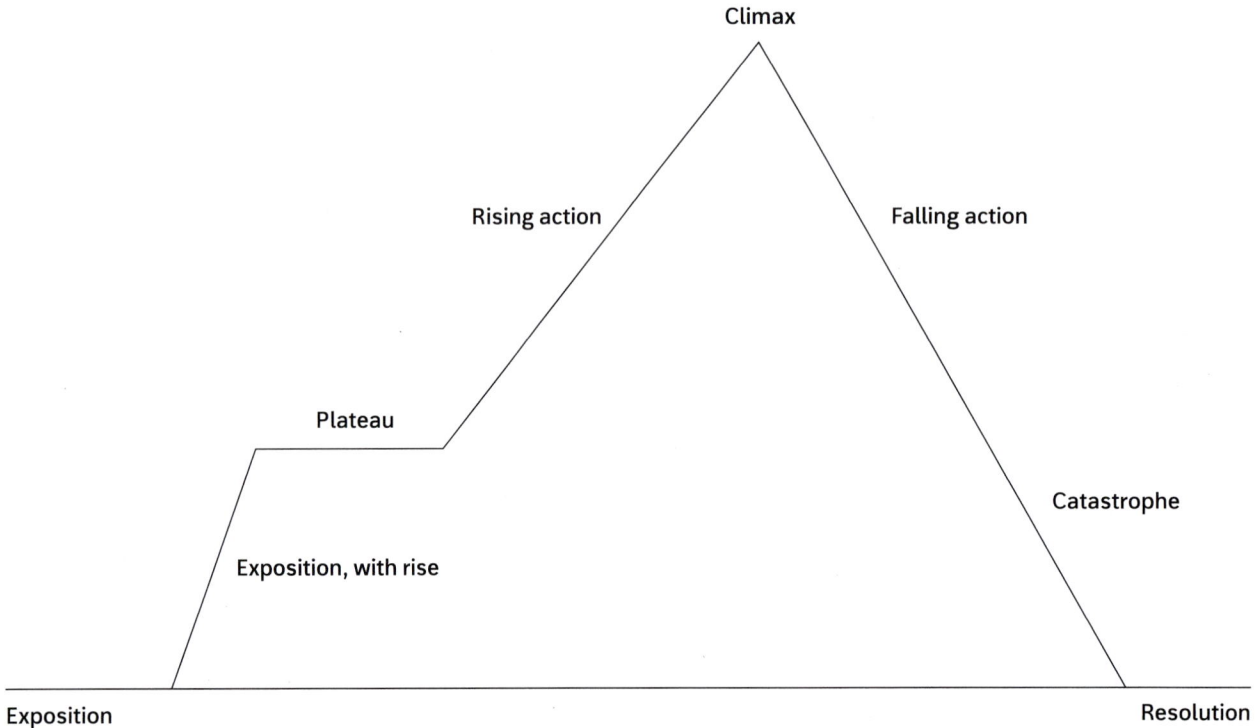

1. **Tick the eight relevant headings which help to structure the plot and add them to the diagram.**
   ☐ Introducing Walt Kowalski and the Lor Family
   ☐ Walt gets dragged into Thao's quarrel with his cousin's gang
   ☐ Walt defends his property against Spider's gang
   ☐ Thao and the Hmong community make amends
   ☐ Walt attacks Smokie for harassing Thao, in retaliation the gang shoots the Lors' house and beats Sue nearly to death
   ☐ Walt decides to take revenge for Sue
   ☐ Walt sacrifices himself when confronting the gang
   ☐ The gang members are arrested, Thao and Sue are safe
   ☐ Walt goes to confession
   ☐ Thao works for Walt
   ☐ Walt is hailed as the neighbourhood's hero

2. **Add three pieces of information to each heading to specify what is going on in the respective situation. Compare with a partner and agree.**

© Westermann Gruppe
Best.-Nr. 041295

Character constellation in *Gran Torino*

The film *Gran Torino* features three main characters and a few minor characters. These characters are exposed to conflicts and problems regarding their family or their neighbourhood. They compare or contrast with one another in reaction to these conflicts.

Having watched the movie…

1. assign the role name to the actors given beneath and add a line explaining who they are. You can do an internet search and add more pictures/characters.
2. cut them out and take turns with another student presenting their story as it is told in the movie.
3. create character constellations for the three main characters to illustrate their importance, development and change in relationships during the plot based on…
   a) the difference between protagonist, antagonist and minor character (type size, colour);
   b) sympathies and antipathies among characters (reflected in distance and closeness);
   c) action and reaction to one another; collaboration/support and rejection/conflict compared to (detailed on arrows).
4. let other students explain a constellation you created to see whether it is comprehensible.

_____

_____

_____

_____

_____

_____

_____

_____

_____

The funeral service/The post-service reception
(scenes 1 + 2, 00:00:50 – 00:09:35)

Watch the opening scene of the film *Gran Torino* and fill in the following graphic to explain how Walt reacts to the people who have come to the memorial service and how they react to him. Then describe Walt in five sentences. (You can use the back of this copy.)

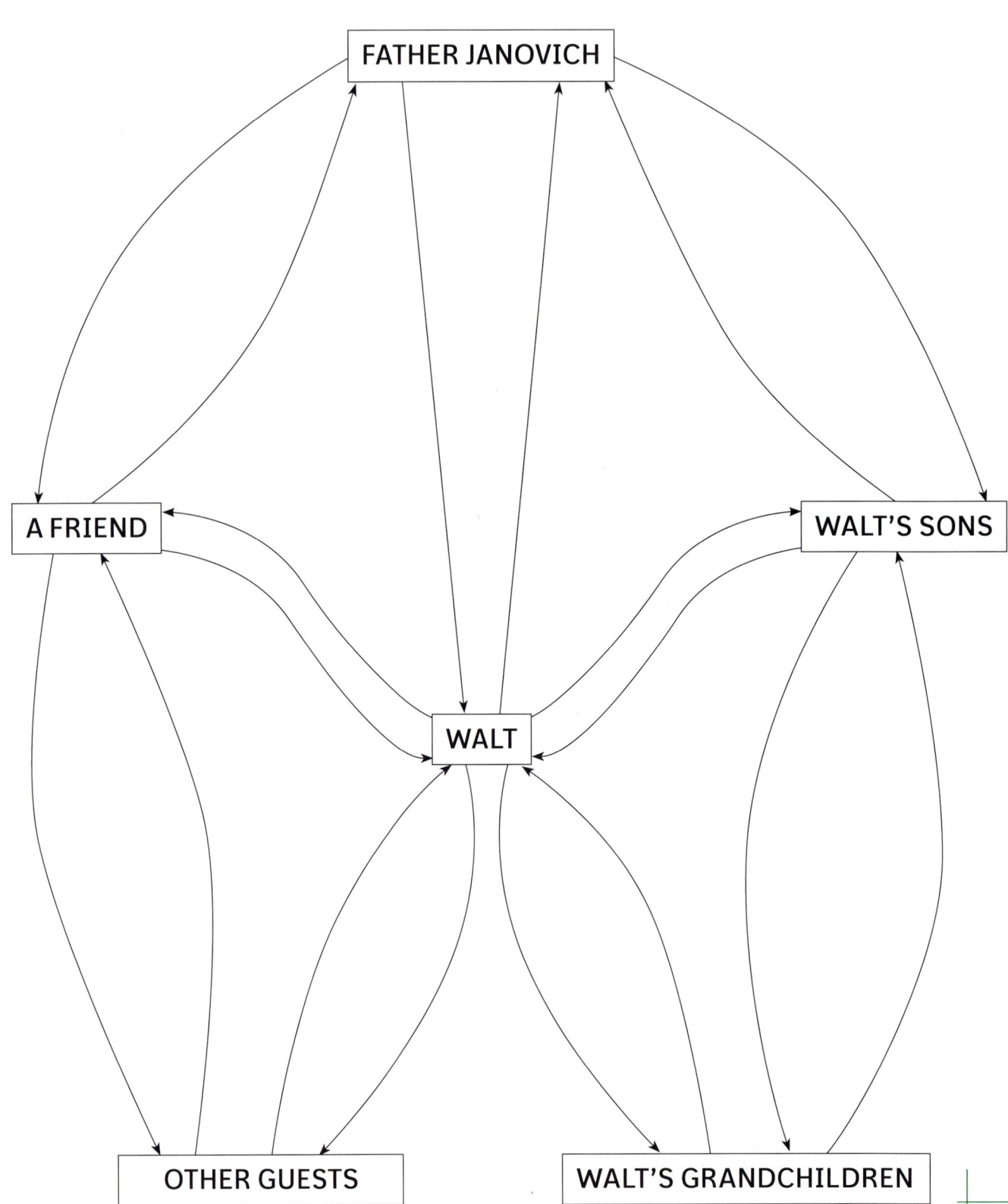

© Westermann Gruppe
Best.-Nr. 041295

The funeral service/The post-service reception
(scenes 1 + 2, 00:00:50 – 00:09:35)

1. At the reception in Walt's home many people mingle. Observe with whom Walt interacts and how he reacts to the different people. What could be his reasons?
   Use as many expressions from the box below as possible.

2. When finished discuss with a partner whether you can sympathize with Walt or whether you find his behaviour inappropriate. Write down your conclusion.

Walt's interaction with/reaction to	(whom Walt interacts with/ reacts to)	possible reason
	the guests at the reception	
	his son Steve	
	his grandsons	
	Mitch, Karen, Ashley	
	people pouring into the neighbours' house	
	Ashley	
	Thao	
	Father Janovich	
	his son Mitch, Karen	

My comment on Walt's behaviour:

• agree only reluctantly	• give up	• roll one's eyes
• be cornered by	• ignore keep busy	• sideswipe sb. slam the door in sb.'s face
• be left thoughtful	• keep one's distance	
• correct sb.	• make a racist remark	• snap at sb.
• dart a look at sb.	• make a saucy comment	• spit out in front of
• eat, drink, talk	• mutter under one's breath	• take sth. calmly
• get rid of sb.	• overhear	• try and make conversation
• get worked up	• pass by without a comment	• turn away frustrated
• give in	• pull oneself together	• turn away sb. harshly
• give sb. a baleful glance	• reply with an ironic undertone	• use a racial slur at
• give sb. a hard look		

Barbarians

A celebration of life (scene 3, 00:09:35 – 00:11:52)

When Walt sees the ritual sacrifice of a chicken in his neighbour's garden he mutters "Damn barbarians". The scene that follows offers a first glimpse into the world of these people.

1. Watch the scene to point out the reason for this ritual.

2. To agree with or reject Walt's comment think about the following aspects. Tick the correct statement. Justify your choice.
    a) In respect of furnishing, Walt's house and the Lors' house are

        ☐ similar.

        ☐ different.

        ☐ incomparable.

    b) The definition of 'masculinity' in Walt's world compared to in the Hmong world is

        ☐ similar.

        ☐ different.

        ☐ incomparable.

    c) The way people celebrate life and death in each household is

        ☐ similar.

        ☐ different.

        ☐ incomparable.

3. Observe how the scene is framed. Explain why the movie director chose to show the contrast between the interior of the Lor family's home and the exterior of Walt's house in this way.

4. The mutual antagonism of Walt and Phong shows in words and in gestures. Put their words into the larger context of the motivation they have and describe the gestures and their effect.

© Westermann Gruppe
Best -Nr. 041295

I'm just calling to ...

A father-son conversation (scene 10, 00:22:07 – 00:23:13)

Match the words of the telephone conversation between Walt and his son Mitch to the cinematic means used (facial expression, gestures, tone of voice or other).

1. "[MITCH:]
   Morning, Dad, it's your number one son, Mitch."

2. "[WALT:]
   It's one in the afternoon."

3. "[MITCH:]
   Right, good afternoon, then."

4. "[WALT:]
   So, what do you want?"

5. "[MITCH:]
   Me? Nothing. What would I want?"

6. "[WALT:]
   I don't know. Your wife already went through all of your mother's jewelry."

7. "[MITCH:]
   No. I was just wondering how you are, what's going on, anything new in the old neighborhood?"

8. "[WALT:]
   Yeah, no."

9. "[MITCH:]
   Great. Smooth sailing then?"

10. "[WALT:]
    Ya."

11. "[MITCH:]
    Okay, good then. Oh, hey, say, Dad?"

12. "[WALT:]
    Yeah."

13. "[MITCH:]
    Do you still know that guy from the plant who has Viking season tickets?"

a) exaggeratedly casual

b) tone of his voice tense

c) a painful pause in the conversation

d) looking at the bullet hole in his Hamm's Beer sign.

e) drumming his fingers on the counter, then walking to and from

f) snapping at the other with sarcasm

g) exasperated sigh, making conversation

h) answering the phone briefly although he knows who is on the other end

i) grimacing

j) grimacing, false chuckle, caught red-handed

k) checking his watch, lashing out in a schoolmasterly tone

l) monosyllabic

m) preoccupied with the true cause for his call

n) raising his eyebrows

o) hesitant

Boo-ga, Boo-ga

A lesson in Hmong (scene 17, 00:36:06 – 00:38:20)

Sue realizes that Walt does not know anything about their culture. She decides to teach him a lesson.

> **1.** Situate the scene into the context of the film.
>
> **2.** While watching the scene work on the following assignments.

1. **Walt's perception of Sue. Tick the correct statements.**

   Walt's words show that he believes

   ☐ that ethnicity and intelligence relate.

   ☐ in cross-culture relationships.

   ☐ that ethnic belonging corresponds with geographic location.

   ☐ migration only brings negative consequences for both the migrants and the country they come to.

2. **Hmong**
   a) Hmong is _____ _____, not a _____.

   b) The Hmong are _____ _____.

   c) They come from different parts in _____, _____ and _____.

   d) During the _____ War they fought on the side of the _____ . They

   came to the US with the help of the _____ Church when

   _____

   _____ .

   e) Hmong girls seem to _____

   whereas boys _____ .

3. **Sue teaching a lesson: Tick the expressions which accurately describe Sue in this scene and explain by continuing the sentence.**

   Sue seems

   ☐ upset about …

   ☐ patient with …

   ☐ tense …

   ☐ ironic …

   ☐ in the picture …   when she/Walt …

   ☐ irritated …

   ☐ impatient …

   ☐ aggressive …

   ☐ empathetic towards …

   ☐ surprised at …

© Westermann Gruppe
Best.-Nr. 041295

Birthday presents for Walt (scene 19, 00:40:11 – 00:42:12)

1. Bring the following comments made by either Mitch or Karen into their correct chronological order to show their goal and line of argumentation. There are two comments which do not come up in the movie. Can you guess which?

   ☐ "You're here all alone."

   ☐ "People there are like you, active and alert, but are alone and would benefit from being around folks their own age."

   ☐ "There's nothing wrong with making things a little less hard on yourself."

   ☐ "We miss Momma, don't we, Daisy?"

   ☐ "With Mom gone, there's got to be a lot to maintain around here, let alone clean."

   ☐ "Of course we're always here for you, Dad."

   ☐ "They have wonderful stores. You can buy new shoes."

   ☐ "There are these great places now, you know, these communities where you don't have to be worrying about mowing the lawn or shoveling snow."

   ☐ "You've worked hard your whole life maybe it's time you started thinking about taking it easier."

   ☐ "They are top-notch, like resorts. It's like staying in a hotel practically."

   ☐ "Another thing, Dad, you really should get rid of the coffin nails."

   ☐ "We were not sure what to get you for your birthday?"

2. Observe how cinematic techniques (medium shots, close-ups, tracking shots, zooming in) support …

   ● Mitch and Karen's intensifying pressure on Walt
   ● Walt's growing irritation
   ● the balance of power between the three of them

3. With a partner discuss the absurdity of the presents Mitch and Karen bring to Walt:

   ● *Happy Birthday Dad* icing on the cake (hypocritical approach)
   ● a big-button phone, despite Walt's sharp eye and obviously good hearing
   ● a gopher (a retrieving tool), neatness of his home and garden, precise movements

As they say, when in Hmong ...

A second birthday (scene 20, 00:42:12 – 00: 53:48)

It's Walt's birthday. Walt has just thrown out Mitch and his wife after they suggested he should move to an old folk's home. Now he is sitting on his porch drinking beer, his dog Daisy at his side.

1. Explain what the introductory sentence of the scene, "We miss Momma, don't we, Daisy?," says about Walt's state of mind.

2. Now watch the beginning of the scene and analyse how Sue is able to persuade Walt to come to the barbecue. Complete the sentences.

   a) Sue approaches Walt like a friend when she ...
   b) She knows that ... can connect people across cultures.
   c) The two are in sync where their ... is concerned.
   d) Her name-calling shows ...
   e) Coincidentally, ...
   f) It is also an opportune moment because Walt ...
   g) Walt's reactions throughout the conversation are ...

3. While watching how Walt experiences the world of the Hmong for the first time, complete the diagram with information on what Walt is doing, what is happening at the barbecue and the change in Walt.

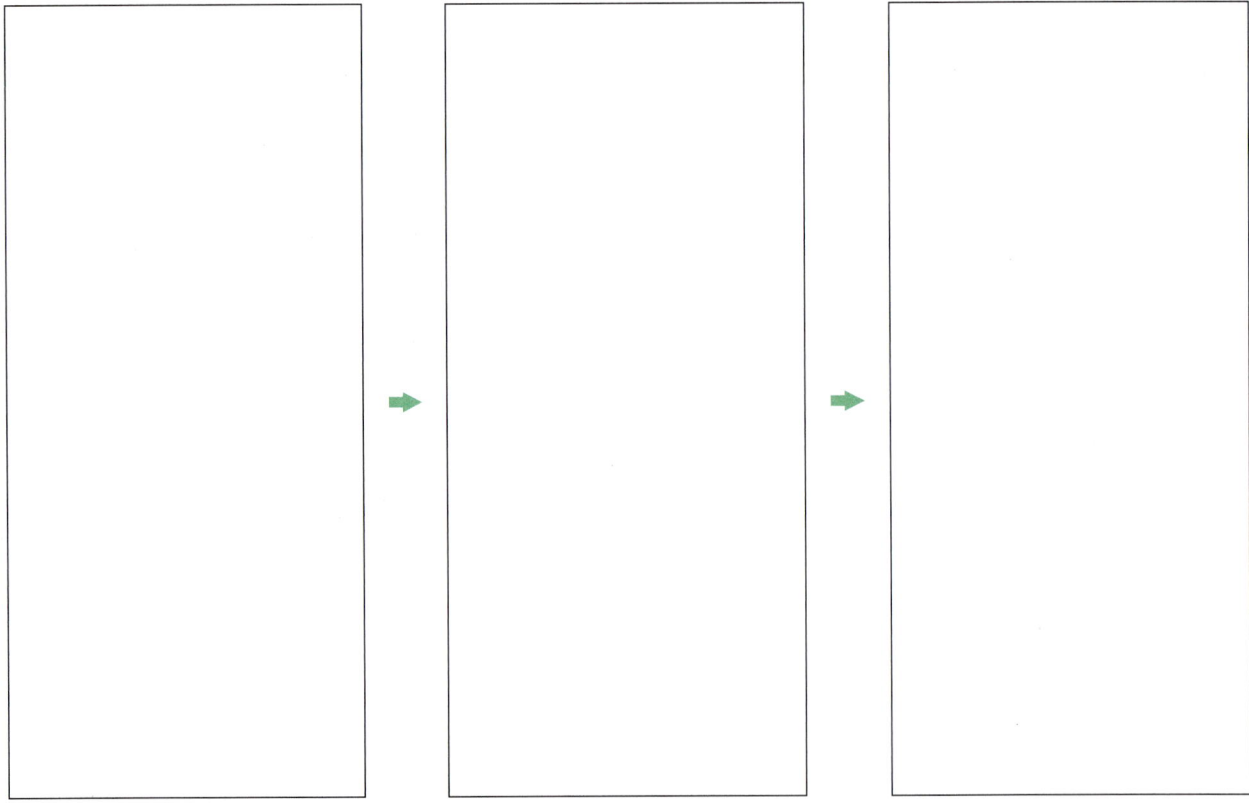

| Walt shows feigned composure and assurance | Walt's epiphany (turning point of the scene) | Walt ... |

© Westermann Gruppe
Best.-Nr. 041295

Growing up Hmong

A role model (scene 29, 1:09:36)

1. Watch the scene from the movie and tick the correct statement.

   The scene above all focuses on

   ☐ Sue by showing her gratitude towards Walt.

   ☐ Walt by stressing the change in him.

   ☐ Thao's chances in life by insisting on the importance of Walt's presence in his life.

2. **Now compare what Sue is saying in the scene to the ideas Nick Schenk originally intended for her to share with Walt in the film script. Tick the ideas which were taken over into the film's dialogue.**

   In the script Sue's words reflect her conviction that …

   ☐ adapting to U.S. culture and society is easier for Hmong girls than for boys.

   ☐ Hmong girls feel more independent than their brothers.

   ☐ they, however, stay close to their mothers and learn from them.

   ☐ Hmong girls take their liberties in dating who they want or in including various aspects of American lifestyle into their daily routines.

   ☐ Hmong boys are not supported enough but left to their own devices.

   ☐ Hmong boys lack orientation.

   ☐ Hmong boys cannot find adequate role models because their fathers have grown up in a different world and cannot give them advice on what to do and who to be in the U.S.

   ☐ seeking guidance they keep to themselves and lose touch with the norms of the old world and the new.

   ☐ many Hmong boys end up in jail.

3. Highlight information characterizing challenges for Hmong teenagers offered in the script.

4. Discuss possible reasons for the difference between film and film script and argue whether you would have done the same.

Talk like a man

Manning Thao up: the right words (scene 31, 1:13:02 – 1:18:42)

Walt wants to 'man Thao up' and takes him to his friend Martin at the barber's shop: "Now you're just gotta learn how guys talk." Watch the scene and analyse the different steps in the process.

1. Walt wants Thao to listen closely to the way men talk.
   Observe their introductory dialogue and tick the correct statements.

   ☐ The message of their conversation is: It's a pleasure to see you.

   ☐ Martin and Walt both use derogatory terms when referring to the other's ethnic background.

   ☐ Their facial expression and gestures contradict their words.

   ☐ Their friendship makes the racial insult ineffective.

2. "You see, kid? Now, that's how guys talk to one another." – "They do?"
   Thao has followed the conversation. Circle the appropriate expression to describe his reaction.

   incredulous – impressed – upset – amused – bewildered

3. Thao's one-to-one imitation of Walt's words – "What's up you old Italian prick?" – fails. Why?

   _____

4. "What should I have said then?" The two men give Thao some instructions for his 'manly talk'. Tick the correct statements.
   Martin and Walt advise Thao to …

   ☐ introduce himself for a start.

   ☐ be respectful of the other person's age and standing.

   ☐ refrain from anything that may insult the person.

   ☐ include some small talk.

   ☐ seek out the other's sympathy by moaning about a problem.

5. In Thao's second attempt he convinces the two men more …

   ☐ with his words.

   ☐ through his body language.

6. Thao applies his newly learnt skills at the construction site: "My head gasket cracked and the goddamned prick at the shop wants to bend me over for $2,100."
   Now, he manages to strike the right note because Kennedy …

   ☐ is sympathetic about his problem with the car.

   ☐ can relate to Thao's problem with the car from his own experience.

   ☐ agrees with Thao in blaming the car mechanics.

© Westermann Gruppe
Best.-Nr. 041295

Violence begets violence

Nothing's fair (scene 39, 1:30:19 – 1:33:23)

Sue has returned home, beaten up and probably raped. Walt is devastated.

1. Add the important stages to the spiral of violence which led to the attack on Sue. Use the diagram below.

2. Analyse the dialogue between Walt and Father Janovich to see how Walt judges the events and who he sees as responsible.

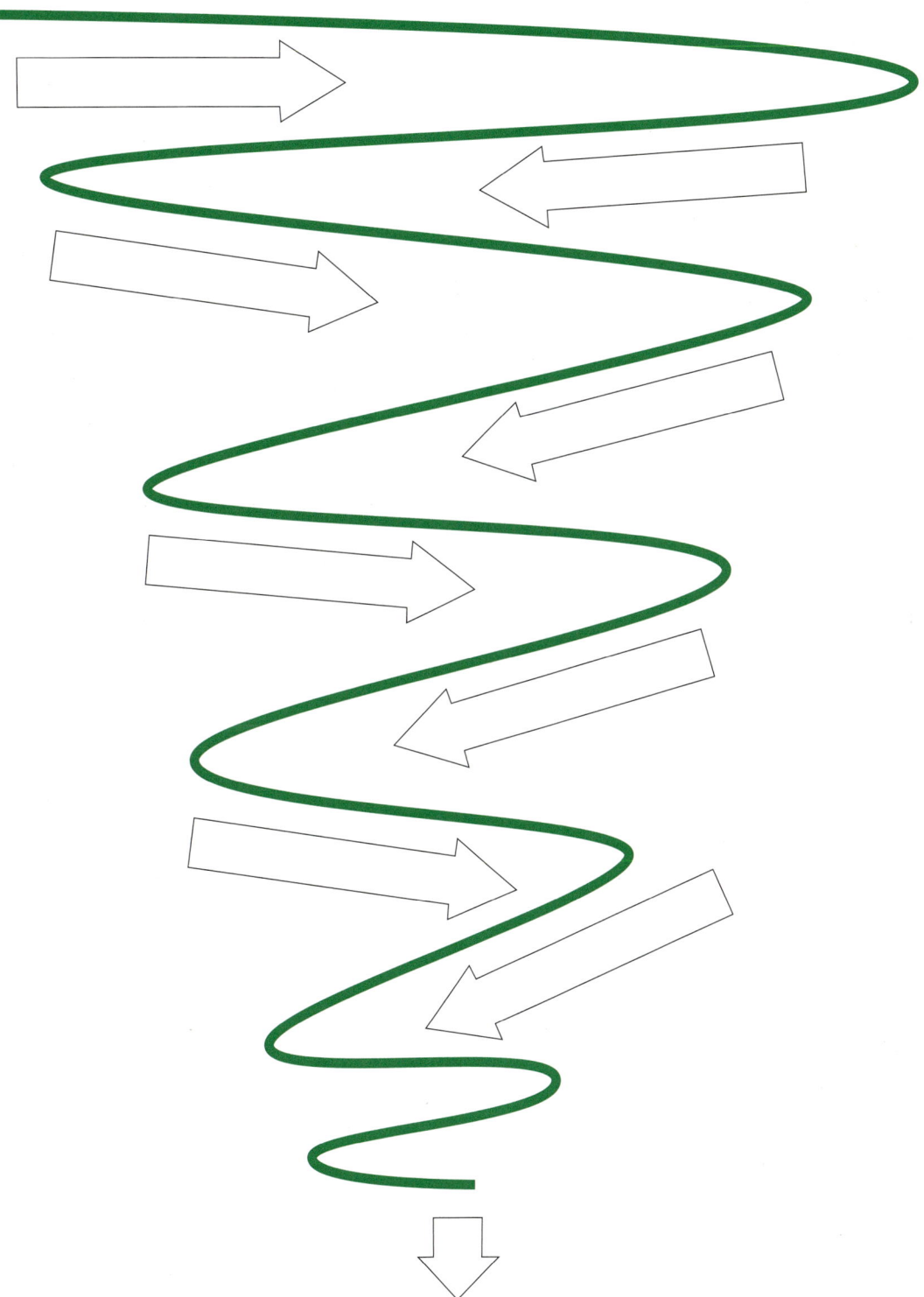

Character frame

Use these templates to gather information on a character.
The questions on the next page may help you to really immerse yourself in him or her.

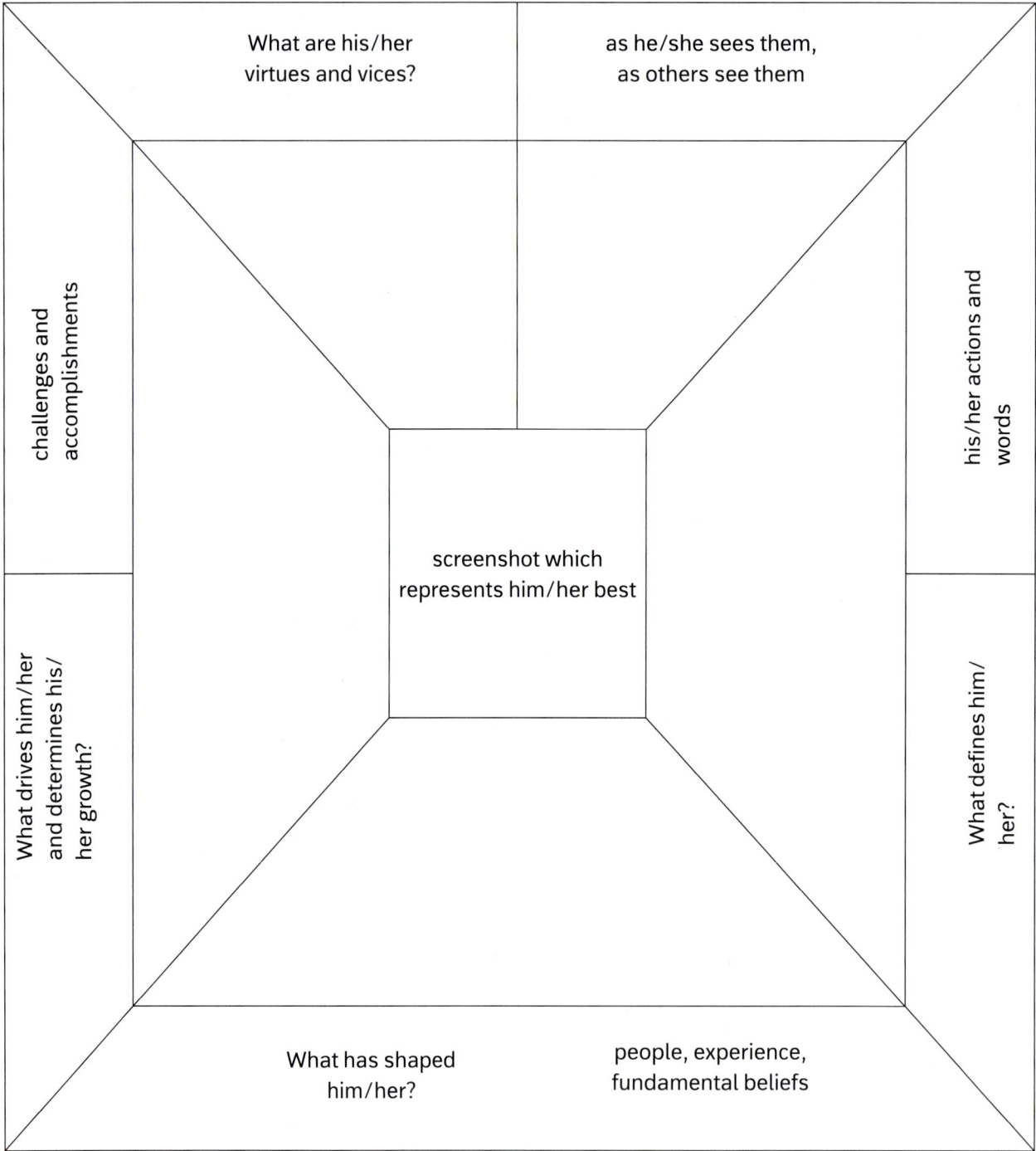

Character frame: Food for thought

Before adding information to the frame, consider some of these aspects.

1. What can be said about the character's …
   - name and nickname?
   - home and location?
   - most striking physical feature?
   - typical posture?
   - favourite objects?

   - likely vocabulary?
   - habits?
   - daily routines?
   - special talents and skills?

2. How does the character relate to …
   - children?
   - parents?
   - friends?
   - neighbours?

   - strangers?
   - successful people?
   - ineffective people?
   - the authorities?

3. What does the character (dis)like most, and why?

4. The character is most (un)comfortable when …

5. How is the character's approach to life? (cautious, brave, reckless …)

6. What does the character most value or prioritize (family, money, success, religion, etc.)?

7. How does the character react to a crisis?

8. What would the character most like to change about her-/himself? Why?

9. What usually causes the problems in the character's life?

10. What (or who) is the character's biggest fear?

11. Does the character hold any prejudices?

12. How does the character think others perceive him or her?

13. Does the character believe in fate or destiny?

14. Whom does the character love best?

15. Who is the most important person in the character's life right now, and why?

16. Is the character generally compassionate or self-involved?

17. Whom does the character most rely on for emotional support?

18. Who is the person who most misunderstands or misjudges the character? Why?

19. Whom does the character most rely on for practical advice?

20. Is the character an optimist or pessimist?

21. What is the character most afraid of?

22. What would the character want to be remembered for?

23. When and how is the character introduced into the film?

24. Which prompts, lighting, or other cinematic devices are used?

25. Which scene with the character is the most memorable in the film?

© Westermann Gruppe
Best.-Nr. 041295

Walt Kowalski: No country for an old man

Auf seiner Veranda weht die amerikanische Flagge, in seiner Auffahrt steht ein Ford Gran Torino, in den er eigenhändig die Lenkung eingebaut hat, in einer Truhe in seinem Keller liegt der ‚Silver Star‘, die Auszeichnung für einen Helden fragwürdiger Taten. Im Zentrum von *Gran Torino* steht Walt Kowalski, alt und krank, verbittert, Idealen vergangener Zeiten verpflichtet. Schmerzlich muss er erkennen, dass seine Welt verloren ist. Das Detroit der 50er-Jahre, das es ihm ermöglichte, durch Fleiß und Moral seinen eigenen kleinen amerikanischen Traum zu leben, für das er in der Fremde tötete, wo er heiratete und eine Familie gründete, gehört nun anderen. Fremde haben es übernommen, die er nicht versteht und die ihn nicht verstehen. Er hat sich zurückgezogen, zeigt wenig Gefühl, spricht nicht mehr als nötig, beobachtet und verurteilt. Distanziert von seinen Söhnen, auf den Hund gekommen, steht er zornig Nachbarn gegenüber, die er für den Verfall seiner Welt verantwortlich macht. Und dennoch wird er am Ende des Films für eben jene Fremde von nebenan sein Leben geben. Mit seinem Gran Torino überantwortet er Thao die Erfahrung seiner Vergangenheit und überträgt damit ihm und nicht seinen eigenen Söhnen die Verantwortung für die Zukunft.

In diesem *Component* lernen die Schülerinnen und Schüler die zentrale Figur des Films kennen, sie verfolgen seinen Erkenntnisprozess, bewerten seine Motive und sein Handeln und versuchen ihn in seiner Komplexität zu begreifen. Sie betrachten das Bedingungsfeld menschlicher Nähe und Zugehörigkeit und beobachten, wie es die Grenzen von Familie, sozialer Schicht und kultureller Herkunft überwinden kann.

In drei Schritten untersuchen sie hierbei die Figur des Walt Kowalski, um seine Entwicklung und seine Entscheidung am Ende verstehen zu können: sie lernen ihn in seinem familiären Umfeld kennen, blicken in seine Vergangenheit, um seine Gegenwart zu begreifen und setzen sich mit seinen Werten und Haltungen auseinander, die ihn zum Außenseiter und Einzelgänger in seiner Umgebung machen.

Die Schülerinnen und Schüler entwickeln in dieser Unterrichtsphase ein *character portrait* (*Copy 15: Character frame*), das sie selbständig und individuell Schritt für Schritt erweitern, am Ende durch den Vergleich mit anderen ergänzen und somit nachhaltig sichern.

2.1 Out of touch with the family

Ziel dieser Sequenz ist es, den Menschen Walt auf der Basis seiner familiären Beziehungen zu ergründen und die Ambiguität von Erwartungen und Erfahrungen innerhalb der Familie als einen Schlüssel zu seiner Persönlichkeit zu begreifen.

Bereits die Eingangsszene des Films zeigt ein umfassendes Bild von Walt Kowalski und seiner Welt. Um die Schülerinnen und Schüler zunächst emotional auf die Szene einzustimmen, werden sie gebeten, sich kreativ auf die Situation der Trauer einzulassen, die den Moment des Gedenkgottesdienstes prägt.

A man (Walt Kowalski) has just lost his wife. They have spent nearly 50 years together.
- How does he most probably feel?
- What does he expect of those who are around him?

- How – according to you – should people react and act in such a situation?
- Which traditions or customs may help to show empathy and support?

In einem Partneraustausch sammeln und bündeln sie spontane Gedanken zu den Fragen und halten im Anschluss individuell ihre Ideen in einem kurzen kreativen Schreibprozess fest. (*Copy 16*). Danach sehen die Schülerinnen und Schüler die Anfangsszene des Films und notieren arbeitsteilig die Reaktionen von Walt und den Menschen, die zum Trauergottesdienst gekommen sind.

We meet Walt Kowalski in a crisis situation. Judging from how he deals with this situation what can we say about him?

Aus den hier angegebenen Musterlösungen können Vokabeln extrahiert werden und als Differenzierungsmaßnahme dem Arbeitsblatt hinzugefügt werden.

Possible solutions:

Walt
- suspiciously eyes the people but his family in particular
- sits in same bench but apart from his family
- seems unemotional when a friend pays his respects
- shows growing irritation towards his grandchildren's behaviour
- does not hide his disapproval of Father Janovich's words

The people gathered at the service
- Father Janovich seems ill at ease when delivering his sermon
- a friend meets the demands of convention by paying Walt his respect on the death of his wife
- Walt's grandchildren fool around or play on their cell phones
- Walt's sons complain about how demanding and unjust their father can be

Im Unterrichtsgespräch werden die Eindrücke gesammelt und vertieft.

- How does Walt's grief show? (e.g. unmoved on the outside, impenetrable glance, in his annoyance against his grandchildren's inappropriate dress and behaviour he grunts and freezes)

- What is the atmosphere like at church? (e.g. gloomy, cold, without comfort)

- What behaviour do you consider inappropriate for the occasion? (e.g. using the cell phone at church, whispering during the sermon, talking badly about a person in mourning)

- Which of the following three expressions best describes the relationship between Walt and his family: distant, estranged, indifferent?

Die letzte Frage wird als Überleitung für die Erarbeitung der Familienkonstellation genutzt, die anhand von vier weiteren Szenen (vgl. z. B. *Copies 6, 8, 10*) analysiert werden soll.
Um die Konsequenzen aus dem zerrütteten Verhältnis von Walt und seiner Familie besser einordnen zu können, wird kurz noch ein *food for thought* in Form einer *4-corner-activity* eingeschoben, das verschiedene Konzeptionen zum Begriff der Familie (*Copy 17*) ins Bewusstsein rückt.
Die Schülerinnen und Schüler werden zunächst gebeten, sich dem Zitat zuzuordnen, dem sie zustimmen.

> Look at the following quotes and decide which one describes your idea of family best. In the group illustrate the statement with examples and come up with a group statement.

Sie erläutern sich das Statement kurz gegenseitig in der Gruppe anhand von Beispielen und formulieren ein Gruppenstatement. Danach werden sie gebeten, das Statement zu wählen, das am ehesten die Situation der Kowalski Familie beschreibt. Im Abgleich zu ihrer eigenen Vorstellung von Familie diskutieren sie in der neuen Gruppe, wie sie das Zusammengehörigkeitsgefühl in dieser Familie bewerten würden.

> Now pick the quote which best describes the state of the Kowalski family. In the group discuss which challenges lie in these specific family ties and who would be responsible for changing things to the better.

Gemeinsam mit den Schülerinnen und Schülern werden Szenen bestimmt, die noch einmal genauer betrachtet werden sollten. In den vorliegenden Erläuterungen werden die Szenen chronologisch bearbeitet, dies ist im Unterricht nicht unbedingt notwendig, sondern kann der Priorisierung der Gruppe angepasst werden. Es müssen auch nicht alle Szenen genutzt werden. Denkbar wäre ebenfalls ein arbeitsteiliges Verfahren im Computerraum oder mit der Hilfe mobiler Endgeräte.

> How can Walt be characterized when we analyse his family relations and compare his reactions to that of those who surround him?

 ## The funeral reception at Walt's home

Nach der Bearbeitung der Filmszene mithilfe von *Copy 6* werden die Ergebnisse über einen *double circle* und im Unterrichtsgespräch weiter vertieft.

> 1. Discuss the following statements (a – g). Back home from church we see Walt among family and friends. We realize that …
>
>   a) Walt is too overwhelmed by the death of his wife to mingle with the guests.
>   b) His sons and their families try hard to be of help and stand by him on this difficult day.
>   c) His grandchildren respect and fear him at the same time.
>   d) Walt shows respect for Father Janovich but feels pressurized by him.
>   e) Walt snaps at the neighbors next door because it is all too much for him.
>   f) His sons are a disappointment to Walt.
>   g) On this day Walt must be forgiven anything because he is in mourning.
>
> 2. According to the presentation in the movie (shots, camera angles, dialogues) who comes across as more likeable, Walt or the other members of his family? Make a ranking.

In der Filmdramaturgie gelingt es dem Regisseur Eastwood Walts Verhalten stets als grenzwertig, aber verständlich zu inszenieren: die Söhne wirken mit ihrem Klagen unreif, Karen überheblich, die Enkel lassen den der Situation angemessenen Anstand vermissen und der junge Priester überfordert in seinem Drängen. Walts karge Worte sind zwar durchsetzt von unangebrachtem Zynismus und derber Fremdenfeindlichkeit, sein Blick aber zeigt seine Verwundbarkeit, seine Haltung, sein Alter und den Schmerz.

Possible solution:
Walt is often depicted towering over people (low angle, coming down the stairs), which stresses his self-righteous behaviour. Confronting people with sarcasm or racist slurs shows how embittered he is, but the viewer can also see reasons for this: his sons seem weak and always complain about how difficult life is for them, his grandchildren are misbehaved teenagers who hold what he owns in higher regard than their grandfather himself (Ashley) and Father Janovich comes on too strong and puts much pressure on a man who has just lost his wife.

Die hier entstandenen Ergebnisse können kurz an der Tafel notiert und im Folgenden weiter ergänzt werden.

I'm just calling to ...

In den beiden Telefongesprächen wird deutlich, wie distanziert das Verhältnis von Walt und seinem Sohn Mitch tatsächlich ist. In der ersten Szene (*Copy 8*) bewertet man die Oberflächlichkeit und Ich-Bezogenheit des Sohnes als grotesk in Anbetracht der Ereignisse der Nacht, muss aber zugeben, dass Mitch aufgrund Walts unnachgiebiger und zynischer Art auch keine Chance bekommt, die Situation richtig einzuschätzen. In der zweiten Szene empfindet man Mitleid mit Walt, dem es einmal mehr nicht gelingt, sich zu öffnen und sich seinem Sohn mitzuteilen und erkennt darin gleichermaßen auch einen Grund für das schwierige Verhältnis von Vater und Sohn:

1. Watch the scene "The line has cut off" (scene 26, 1:00:58 – 1:03:36): Now comment on the telephone conversation between Walt and his son Mitch by putting into words what they are actually saying or trying to say if they had the courage.

2. Let us analyse the relationship between Walt and his son Mitch a little further. How do the two come across in these two scenes?

   a) A father-son conversation (scene 10, 00:22:07 – 00:23:13) (cf. quotes and task on *Copy 8*)
   b) The line has cut off (scene 26, 1:00:58 – 1:03:36) (cf. task 1. above)

Die Zitate aus dem Film und der Arbeitsauftrag auf *Copy 8* bzw. oben werden genutzt, um Vater und Sohn einander gegenüberzustellen und ihr Verhältnis zu bewerten.

Mitch	Walt
<ul><li>insensitive and superficial</li><li>not seriously interested in his father's well-being</li><li>egoistic in pursuing his interests</li><li>easily unsettled by his father's sarcasm</li></ul>	<ul><li>monosyllabic, unwavering, unrelenting</li><li>irritable and snappy in his answers</li><li>judgmental about his son's self-centered and dishonest nature</li><li>unable to open up and express himself</li></ul>

Between Walt and Mitch no genuine and honest communication is possible, because on the one hand Walt keeps his distance and is evasive when it comes to saying what he truly feels and on the other hand Mitch, not having learned to rid himself of his father's resoluteness and rigid views, has become self-absorbed and materialistic.

Birthday presents for Walt

Die letzte hier im Fokus stehende Szene zeigt durch einen Vergleich von Außen- und Innenperspektive die Komplexität der zentralen Figur des Walt Kowalski (*Copy 10*). Die Geschenke von Mitch und Karen gewählt für einen alten, gebrechlichen Mann und ihre Lösungsvorschläge für seinen Lebensabend werden von Walt mit Verachtung und Zorn bestraft, denn seine ausgeprägte Disziplin, seine Energie, sein Kampfesgeist und sein unerschütterlicher Glaube an eine selbstbestimmte unabhängige Existenz lassen ihn Einsamkeit und körperliche Beschwerden verdrängen.

It is true. Walt is old, obviously ill and definitely lonely after the death of his wife. Why then do we as viewers show solidarity with Walt against Mitch and Karen on his birthday?

Possible solution:
The family who is supposed to support him only see him as a burden and want to deport him into an old folk's home to get rid of the responsibility. Walt, however, is still perfectly capable of leading an independent life. Contrary to his family's opinion, he not only fully controls his life but is also able to intervene into the lives of others and help them get along.

Mit diesem Impuls sind die Schülerinnen und Schüler aufgefordert, die Ergebnisse der detaillierten Analyse zusammenfassend zu bewerten. Um nun Walts Reaktion zu verdeutlichen, sollen sie in einem weiteren Schritt seine Gedanken als mögliche Off-Kommentare formulieren.

Reacting to Mitch and Karen's comments (*Copy 10*) create a line of thought for Walt at each step which could be used in a voice-over and which connects the viewer to his immediate reaction.

Possible solution:
I'm not as deadbeat as you think.
What would you know about hard work?
Why the hell should I? As if you cared.
A bit of maintenance work would not do you any harm either.
Better than spending a minute with you lot.
As if that were a problem.
And what exactly should a man be doing there?

Die hier vorgeschlagenen Reaktionen können natürlich auch zur Diskussion genutzt werden, inwiefern ein solches *voice-over* eine Alternative zu dem schweigenden Walt im Film wäre.

What have we learned about Walt Kowalski so far? How does the understanding of Walt's complicated relations with his family contribute to a judgement of his character?

Zum Abschluss dieser Sequenz resümieren die Schülerinnen und Schüler ihre Erkenntnisse, indem sie aus Walts Perspektive so viele Antworten auf die 21 Fragen (*Copy 18*) finden wie möglich und sich Notizen für sein Charakterportrait machen. Der folgende Schreibauftrag rundet diesen Unterrichtsschritt ab.

"Kill you to buy American"

Walt quarrels with a lot that Mitch and his family do. Show how father and son differ in their everyday life to explain the effects of their complicated relationship on each other.

2.2 A stranger in his own neighbourhood

Walt Kowalski sitzt auf seiner Veranda und betrachtet die Nachbarschaft. Während sein Haus noch die Zeichen der ehemals gepflegten Wohngegend zeigt, verfallen die Häuser links und rechts immer mehr. Walt erkennt in seiner Nachbarschaft den Mikrokosmos einer Nation im Zerfall, die er mit seiner Hände Arbeit aufgebaut hat und die er einst mit seinem Leben verteidigte. Voller Vorurteile steht er als Außenseiter am Rande dieser sich wandelnden Gesellschaft, bezeichnet die Hmongs von nebenan als ‚gooks‘, Amerikaner mit italienischen oder irischen Wurzeln als ‚dagos‘ oder ‚paddies‘ und vertritt offensiv die Position, dass man unter seinesgleichen am besten aufgehoben ist.

In dieser Unterrichtssequenz analysieren die Schülerinnen und Schüler die Veränderungen und den Umgang mit Andersartigkeit aus Walts Blickwinkel. Der gesellschaftskritische Ansatz wird erst in *Component 3* vertieft.

Zum Einstieg wird ein *film still* (00:03:52) genutzt, das in einem *long shot* Walts Haus und das der Nachbarsfamilie Lor zeigt. Im *Lend me your eyes*-Verfahren sind die Schülerinnen und Schüler aufgefordert, das *setting* bzw. die Unterschiede zwischen beiden Häusern zu beschreiben.

1. Describe the house and its surroundings in detail.

2. Which assumptions can be made about the inhabitants of the house on the basis of this long shot?

3. Falling back on scenes in the movie what details do you remember about the houses and the way they are maintained?

Possible solution:
3. Walt is mowing the lawn, the tools in his garage show he does repairs on the house and household gadgets, in the Lor house the ventilator is broken, they need a new refrigerator, Thao clears the garden of weeds

Im Anschluss wird das Bild als Ganzes gezeigt und auf die Bildsprache verwiesen:

If you analyse this shot from a director's point of view, what is its significance?
Possible solution:
- the long shot and the lighting make a confrontation between the houses possible
- the angle allows the viewer to also see Walt's garage entrance and garage in which he keeps his Gran Torino
- the lamp post symbolizes the border between two worlds

Die daran anschließenden Szenen zeigen, was in beiden Häusern zur gleichen Zeit vor sich geht. Während in Walts Haus die Trauer um seine Frau die Menschen zusammenbringt, feiert die Lor-Familie die Ankunft eines neuen Lebens (siehe *Copy 7*). In dieser Szene spiegeln sich die ersten Gemeinsamkeiten und Unterschiede im Alltagsleben der beiden Kulturen.

In the plot of the movie this shot shows not only two houses but introduces two scenarios within them. Whereas in Walt's house people gather to mourn the death of his wife, his neighbours celebrate a different occasion.
Which similarities and differences can you make out in these two cultures?

Possible solution:
There are more similarities than differences. Both houses look rather the same

> from the inside; in both cultures the cliché that men are the head of the household and superior to women seems prevalent; the beginning and the end of someone's life is considered a reason to invite people over and feed them, both occasions are accompanied by a spiritual guide or leader. Some traditions and rites differ. The movie ironically equates Walt's snappy comments with Phong's angry tirade, their spitting included.

Noch weiß Walt davon nichts, er wird aber eine ähnliche Situation an seinem Geburtstag kennenlernen und verstehen, wie wenig sich seine Nachbarn von ihm unterscheiden. Zunächst wird er aber in seinen Vorurteilen bestärkt. Das Nachbargrundstück ist verwahrlost, Thao versucht, ihn zu bestehlen, und er wird in die Auseinandersetzung mit der Gang hineingezogen.

- Walt on the contrary only sees his neighbours as intruders disturbing his peace and quiet. Which scenes illustrate this?
- When does his perception change? Whom does he relate to first and why?

Possible solution:
First he observes Sue courageously defending herself against the black gang, then he sees how Thao helps a neighbour and picks up her groceries. Courage and the willingness to help are two traits Walt values in people.

Sue, klug und spontan, schreckt nicht vor ihm zurück, sondern beeindruckt ihn durch ihren Wagemut. Sie unterstützt Walts Umdenkprozess (*Copy 11*).

On his birthday Walt finally comes face to face with Hmong hospitality and learns a lesson for life. First observe how he is persuaded by Sue, then see how Walt reacts to what he experiences in the Lor house. How does this change him?

Dieser Tag hat Walts Einstellung zu seinen Nachbarn verändert, und er überdenkt seine Rolle. Seine Welt zerfällt zwar nach wie vor in Gut und Böse und in Richtig und Falsch, aber die Lor-Familie zählt nun zu dem, was es zu verteidigen gilt. In einer *ranking-activity* bewerten die Schülerinnen und Schüler Walts Werte. Dies kann arbeitsteilig geschehen. Die eine Hälfte der Gruppe beschäftigt sich mit den positiven Werten, die andere mit den Charakterschwächen, die Ergebnisse werden argumentiert vorgestellt und gemeinsam an der Tafel gesammelt, um dann Zuordnungen vornehmen zu können.

1. The Lors are no longer the enemy but will become part of what Walt is ready to support and defend. Let us reconsider what he believes in, what he appreciates in some people and what makes him despise others. Rank the following ideas in order of importance for Walt to identify 'friend and foe' in his world.
   - sincerity
   - hard work
   - self-reliance and autonomy
   - respect for the other
   - integrity and responsibility
   - people with substance
   - taking care of things
   - courage
   - selflessness
   - self-respect
   - incompetence
   - laziness, uselessness
   - harassment and violence
   - empty rhetoric
   - disregard and neglect
   - self-pity
   - inappropriate language or behavior
   - whining and looking for excuses
   - greed and avarice
   - privileges

2. If these characteristics are applied to Sue and Thao on the one hand and to his sons, their wives and his grandchildren on the other who would give a better account of themselves?

Das Ergebnis dieses Vergleichs liefert Walt Argumente für die Regelung seines Nachlasses. Aus ehemaliger Feindschaft und Abwehr entsteht aufrichtige Zuneigung und erwächst Walts Bereitschaft, diese Menschen an geordnete amerikanische Zustände und Werte wie Leistungsorientierung und Effizienz heranzuführen. Thaos Frondienst kommt ihm da gerade recht. In einer Partneraktivität listen die Schülerinnen und Schüler Walts Maßnahmen auf, mit denen er ans Werk geht.

Walt has come to understand and participate in the cultural ways of his neighbours and now sees it his duty to teach them about the American ways. Take turns in naming measures Walt depicts to kill two birds with one stone: support and defend his neighbours and at the same time restore his neighborhood to its former glory.

Possible solution:
Walt instructs Thao about respect and teaches him how to stand up for himself without violence and become more than what people expect of him. He puts Thao to work fixing up the neighbourhood. He finds him honest work: a manual job on a construction site. He admonishes Sue for verbal misdemeanor, which is incompatible with her role as a young woman. He takes risks by not only defending the two adolescents against gang violence but also by boldly following his plan through to put an end to the gang forever.

Die Dimension seines Vorhabens zeigt sich zu allererst in seiner Erkenntnis am Ende, dass diese Aufgabe nur durch den Einsatz seines Lebens gelöst werden kann. Allerdings spiegelt eine Szene den minimalen Radius von Walts Bemühen bereits vorab. Die Schülerinnen und Schüler ergründen die Funktion dieser Szene, indem sie zunächst den *tracking shot* im Warteraum der Arztpraxis (1:01:04 – 1:01:26) kreativ ergänzen. Der Film wird immer wieder angehalten, um die fokussierten Personen auszudeuten: Woher könnten sie kommen, welche Sprache sprechen sie, welche Aspekte ihrer Kultur weichen von der amerikanischen *mainstream culture* ab, welche Vorurteile könnten ihnen begegnen?

1. Walt's endeavor is progressing. Not only the facades in the neighbourhood are changing but also the people, as they seem to grow closer together. Then Walt has another coughing fit and goes to see a doctor. What does he notice in the waiting room?

2. Together with a partner speculate about the people around Walt: Where might they come from? What languages do they speak? Are there any cultural differences to mainstream America? What prejudice might they encounter?

3. Why was this scene integrated in the film?

Walt lässt dennoch in seinem Bemühen nicht nach und am Ende steht für Sue und Thao die Zukunft offen – Spiders Gang wird abgeführt. Doch was hat sich tatsächlich verändert? Die Schülerinnen und Schüler analysieren und bewerten Walts Selbstaufopferung mithilfe einer *good-angel-bad-angel activity*.

1. Even if his cause is overwhelming, in the defence of Sue and Thao and his crusade against the decay in the old neighbourhood Walt is prepared to go to extremes. He sacrifices his life. Can we follow his reasoning?

2. A third of the group will come up with 3–5 reasons which speak in favour of Walt's choice, another third thinks of 3–5 reasons which speak against it. The last third reflects on two quotes to decide which one Walt would have embraced:
   "Heroism is accessible. Happiness is more difficult." (Albert Camus)
   "Heroism often results as a response to extreme events." (James Geary)

3. In groups of three discuss the reasons speaking in favour of or against Walt's self-sacrifice. Using one of the quotes present your findings and explain whether you consider Walt's deed heroic or not.

Den Abschluss dieser Sequenz bildet wieder ein Schreibprodukt:

Choose one of the quotes from the film and explain how they relate to Walt and his situation.

"[WALT, reading out his horoscope:] 'Your birthday today; This year you have to make a choice between two life paths. Second chances come your way. Extraordinary events culminate in what might seem to be an anti-climax.'"

"[SUE, translating the shaman's words:] Kor Khue says that you think you've been disrespected. You do not live your life. Your food has no flavor. You are scared of your past. You stopped living years and years ago. Kor Khue says you're not at peace."

"[WALT, reacting to what he experiences in his neighbours' home:] Son of a bitch. I've got more in common with these goddamned gooks than my own spoiled-rotten family."

2.3 A relic of distant times

Walt Kowalski scheint gleichermaßen aus der Zeit gefallen und doch in ihr unbeirrbar präsent und konsequent dynamisch. Nostalgisch aber nicht sentimental spiegelt sich in seinem Haus und seinen Autos der Zeitgeist der 50er-Jahre. Seine Auffassungen sind dementsprechend konformistisch traditionell, er lebt die konservativ-bürgerlichen Werte dieser Zeit: Kleinfamilie und Eigenheim in den „suburbs", materieller Wohlstand und Fortschrittsglaube, strebsam und unauffällig, was sich z. B. in diesem Zitat ausdrückt: „Well … I survived the war … got married … and raised a family." Das positive Selbstbild der wirtschaftlich und militärisch zur Supermacht avancierten Vereinigten Staaten erzeugte gleichermaßen neue Vorurteile und Abgrenzungsverhalten. Neben der noch andauernden Segregation stärkte der politisch forcierte Anti-Kommunismus in der weißen Mittelschicht das Misstrauen in alles Fremde, das durch persönlich-individuelle Kriegserfahrung krude Bestätigung findet. Walts Seele leidet unter traumatischen Erfahrungen im Koreakrieg, die in einem Klima gesellschaftlicher Ignoranz und daraus resultierender individueller Überforderung nie aufgearbeitet wurden.

In dieser Sequenz erkennen die Schülerinnen und Schüler wodurch Walts Haltungen geprägt und wie seine Handlungsweisen motiviert sind.

Zum Einstieg reflektieren die Schülerinnen und Schüler folgenden Austausch zwischen Walt und Sue und äußern ihre Assoziationen (*Copy 19*):

"I'm old school." – "Yeah, but you're American."

1. Would you agree with Sue and Walt? How does the movie transport the idea that Walt is an 'old school American'?

Possible solution:
his strict morals, the American flag waving from his porch, his well-maintained property, the Gran Torino, his handling of firearms, etc.

2. Let us take a look at how the time frame of the 1950s shaped some of these traits and his way of acting.

Mithilfe von *Copy 20* lernen die Schülerinnen und Schüler im Folgeschritt prägende Aspekte der 50er-Jahre kennen und spüren diese in Walts Gegenwart wieder auf. Das Setting von Walts Haus und die Pflege seines Gran Torino zeigen, wie sehr sich Walt den Geist der 50er-Jahre bewahrt hat und durch ihn geprägt ist.

Find out how the spirit of the 1950s seems still alive in Walt's world of the 21st century.

Possible solutions:
Walt worked in the booming automobile industry, he lived in the suburbs with his family, he keeps the spirit of the 50s alive by sticking to his Gran Torino, he defends his idea of 'America' with a gun if necessary, his mindset still shows the concept that ethnic groups better not mix …

To further investigate Walt's mindset and understand what makes him tick, we must focus on another reality of the 1950s.

Die Überleitung zu Walts Koreaerfahrungen gestaltet sich mit dem *screenshot* (00:04:03), der das Bild zeigt. Die Signatur des Bildes „Third Platoon, E company, March second, 1952, Korea" und die Frage des einen Jungen: „Where's Korea?" werden über die Untertitel mit eingeblendet und als Impuls aufgegriffen, um das Vorwissen der Schülerinnen und Schüler abzufragen:

What are the boys looking at? What do you know about Korea, then and now?

In einem *flash light* werden Assoziationen festgehalten und nach dem Lesen eines Hintergrundtextes (*Copy 21*) ergänzt. Hierzu ergibt sich möglicherweise ein Tafelbild wie folgt:

Possible solution:
The Allies of WW II liberated Korea from Japanese occupation and separated the country along the 38th parallel (north) into a communist North Korea under the influence of the Soviet Union and a capitalist South Korea under the influence of the United States.

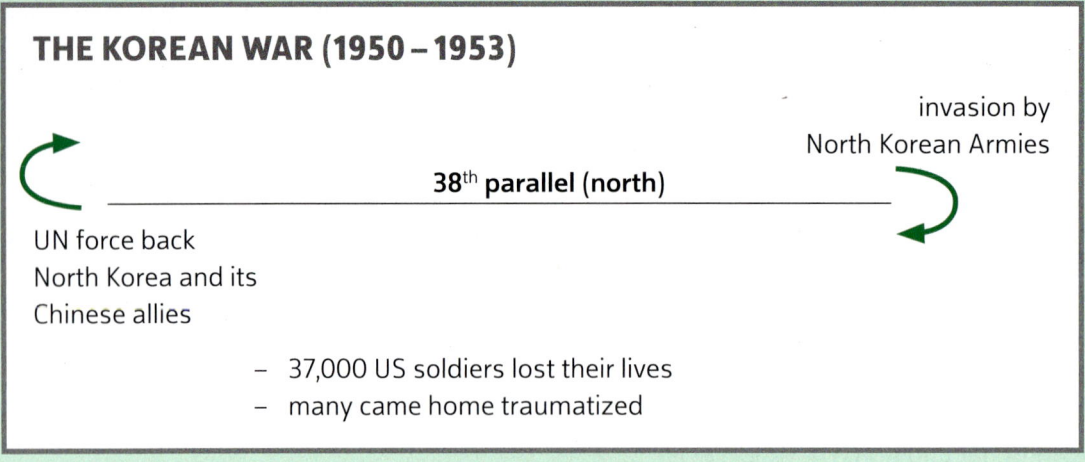

THE KOREAN WAR (1950 – 1953)

invasion by
North Korean Armies

38ᵗʰ parallel (north)

UN force back
North Korea and its
Chinese allies

– 37,000 US soldiers lost their lives
– many came home traumatized

Um die psychologischen Auswirkungen der Kriegserfahrung und Walts Worte im Film besser einschätzen zu können, werden diese faktischen Informationen nun an persönlichen Realitäten gebrochen.

Dies geschieht über Zitate eines Dokumentarfilms (*Copy 22*), dessen Trailer auf YouTube zu finden ist. Vorsicht! Der Trailer selbst ist nur bedingt für das Klassenzimmer geeignet, da er drastisches Bildmaterial enthält. Die Aussagen der Kriegsveteranen aber bieten einen Einblick in die menschliche Seele und füllen Walts eher karge Worte etwas auf.

> What do the quotes tell us about the challenges the soldiers faced during the operation?
>
> **Possible solutions:**
> They had to …
> ● act on order without objecting
> ● control their fears to survive
> ● be ready to give their lives
> ● force themselves to kill
> ● …

Nun wird der Fokus wieder zurück auf den Film gelenkt und Walts Verhalten und seine Reaktionen im Hinblick auf seine Kriegserfahrung betrachtet. Die folgenden Kriterien können per Folie projiziert und so nachhaltiger diskutiert werden.

> Military training and wartime experience shape the soldier's mind.
> Very often veterans are said to …
> ● be able to perform in stressful situations
> ● stick to schedules and routines easily
> ● make decisions quickly and take responsibility for their actions
> ● value respect and professionalism
> ● usually be able to communicate clearly and efficiently
> ● show problem-solving abilities
> ● follow their tasks through all the way to the end
>
> Which of these traits also apply to Walt and can be explained through his past as a Korean War veteran? What else have you observed that may be related back to his days as a soldier?

Possible solution:
swearing and cussing, handling his problems with a gun, ordering people around, avoiding unnecessary words, unemotional approach to things and people

Außer diesen antrainierten Eigenschaften zeigen sich aber auch Auswirkungen einer traumatischen Erfahrung bei Walt (*Copy 23*). Dies soll nun anhand der diesbezüglich relevanten Filmszenen erarbeitet werden.

Father Janovich insists that Walt's wife wanted him to go to confession. The viewer soon realizes that this may have something to do with the war, too. Let us find out what exactly has traumatized Walt and how he deals with it.

Diese Phase kann bei einem möglichen Einsatz von mehreren mobilen Endgeräten wieder arbeitsteilig organisiert werden, indem sich fünf Gruppen intensiv mit jeweils einer der relevanten Szenen auseinandersetzen und ihr Ergebnis dann im Plenum präsentieren bzw. zu einem Gesamtergebnis (Tafelanschrieb oder Lösungsblatt) zusammenfügen.

Possible solution:

Unscrupulously Walt is ready to go to all extremes in a confrontation: His war experience has taught him not to see the human in the one he killed and so the act of killing has in return dehumanized himself.

Resigned, Walt does not believe in the institutions of a civil society anymore: In the war he learned to trust only in himself, to take things into his own hands and not to bank on anyone else.

Traumatizing incident: **Walt killed a Korean youth** **who was ready to surrender**

Resolved to carry his guilt alone Walt believes he is unaccountable to anyone: He has found a way to redemption and to reconcile the fate of the youth he killed in Vietnam with his own death.

Incredulously Walt refutes the opinion of others: Life and death are inextricably interwoven; they cannot be learned 'second hand' but must be experienced.

Upright in the face of his deed Walt has chosen to become the master of his own fate: He believes he overstepped the bounds of duty during the war and therefore is lost forever.

Absolutely determined, Walt goes his own way to the very end: He is ready to sacrifice his life for Thao and his sister in the hope that he can thereby finally make amends for his shameful deed in Korea.

Nachdem die Schülerinnen und Schüler erkennen konnten, wie Walt durch sein Erleben des Krieges in Korea geprägt ist, sind sie nun abschließend aufgefordert, Walts Verhalten in der Gegenwart zu bewerten. Mithilfe einer *positioning-line* oder einem *double circle* betrachten sie einzelne Aspekte.

Now that we have seen how Walt Kowalski has been shaped through his experience in the war, let us examine his final decision and act. Assess the following statements about Walt, illustrate the statements through scenes in the movie and discuss alternatives for Walt with other students near you.

- It is admirable to observe Walt, a real man and a hard-boiled survivor, take whatever life threw at him and keep marching.
- It is a shame that protecting and keeping his Gran Torino in shape is Walt's sole tangible link to a past where life seemed worthwhile.
- Walt is to be pitied because he has survived an extremely difficult life to arrive in times which hold no meaning for him.
- Since Walt had to pay dearly for what little he has, he is right in despising those who do not do anything or make anything.
- Walt correctly judges others on the basis of their own demonstrated merit.
- It makes Walt strong that he does what he feels is best, and not what will endear him to others.
- Walt has always done what was expected of him – now the time is right to follow his instincts.
- Walt knows that he is nearing the end of his life and that this sacrifice is the only means to give his life some worthwhile meaning.
- Walt remains true to the man he always was; he was a hero in life, and becomes a hero in death.

Das letzte Statement kann für eine kreative Schreibproduktion genutzt werden: Die Schülerinnen und Schüler schreiben einen Nachruf auf Walt, indem sie die Betrachtungen der Stunde mit einfließen lassen und auf folgende Fragen eine Antwort finden.

"In loving memory"

Write an epitaph for Walt Kowalski. Include your answers to the following questions:
- Who was Walt Kowalski? (e.g. a husband and father, a mechanic, a ...)
- What made Walt special?
- What will the world be without Walt Kowalski?

In mourning: Working words

Use expressions from a word box to make a statement on a topic. Choose one of the forms below.

ACROSTIC			
	L _____	M _____	G _____
	O _____	O _____	O _____
	S _____	U _____	N _____
	S _____	R _____	E _____
		N _____	
		I _____	
		N _____	
		G _____	

Acrostic: a poem in an alphabetic script, in which the first letter or word of each verse in the text spells out another message

HAIKU

_____ (title)

_____ _____ _____ _____ _____

_____ _____ _____ _____ _____ _____ _____

_____ _____ _____ _____ _____

Haiku: a poem composed of three unrhymed lines of five, seven, and five words

DIAMANTE

line 1: subject (one word)
line 2: two adjectives describing the subject
line 3: three words ending in "ing" telling about the subject
line 4: four words, the first two describing the subject, the last two describing its opposite
line 5: three words ending in "ing" telling about the opposite
line 6: two adjectives describing the opposite
line 7: the opposite of the subject (one word)

CINQUAIN

line 1: the title (one word)
line 2: two words that describe the title
line 3: three words that tell the action
line 4: four words that express the feeling
line 5: one word which recalls the title

The idea of family

In every conceivable manner,
the family is link to our past,
bridge to our future.
Alex Haley

I don't care how poor a man is;
if he has family, he's rich.
Dan Wilcox

Family life is not a computer
program that runs on its own; it
needs continual input from everyone.
Neil Kurshan

Families are like fudge – mostly
sweet, with a few nuts.
Les Dawson

Sources: Alex Haley: https://www.brainyquote.com/quotes/alex_haley_391545 [03.05.2018]; Dan Wilcox: https://www.goodreads.com/quotes/271687-i-don-t-care-how-poor-a-man-is-if-he [03.05.2018]; Neil Kurshan: https://www.brainyquote.com/quotes/neil_kurshan_403327 [03.05.2018]; Les Dawson: https://www.goodreads.com/quotes/533350-families-are-like-fudge---mostly-sweet-with-a-few [03.05.2018]

21 questions to Walt

1. What is your favourite occupation?

2. What is your greatest fear?

3. What is your greatest regret?

4. What is your most marked characteristic?

5. What is your motto?

6. What is it that you most dislike?

7. What do you most value in a person?

8. What is the quality you want to see in a man?

9. What is the quality you want to see in a woman?

10. What is the trait you most deplore in others?

11. What is the trait you most deplore in yourself?

12. What occupies your mind most these days?

13. When and where were you happiest?

14. Which person around you do you most admire?

15. Which person around you do you most despise?

16. Which talents do you have?

17. Which words or phrases do you most overuse?

18. If you could change one thing about yourself, what would it be?

19. If you could change one thing in the world, what would it be?

20. What do you consider your greatest achievement?

21. What is your idea of perfect happiness?

© Westermann Gruppe
Best.-Nr. 041295

To be 'old school' – to be American (scene 28, 01:08:58)

1. Discuss with a partner whether the following aspects apply to Walt or not. Rank those which correctly describe Walt to explain what makes him an 'old school American'.

Walt believes in

☐ adhering to strong moral standards   ☐ defending his 'homestead'

☐ keeping things simple   ☐ appearance for respect's sake

☐ structuring his day   ☐ keeping a promise

☐ self-reliance   ☐ his country

☐ self-discipline   ☐ church and government

☐ taking the law in his own hands   ☐ God

☐ maintaining his property   ☐ the saying that blood is thicker than water

☐ doing things like they have always been done

☐ hard work: a man should be diligent, conscientious and honest

2. Here are some informal and pejorative expressions which people may use to show their opinion of people like Walt.
Put yourself into the perspective of Mitch, Karen, Ashley, his grandsons, Thao, his friend the barber, Father Janovich, his neighbours or his friends. Then pick one of the expressions that matches what this person (or people) might think of Walt and explain what makes them think so.

- **broken record:** sb. who annoys others by repeating the same ideas over and over again
- **dinosaur:** sb. who is no longer effective or useful because he is too old-fashioned
- **bore:** sb. who talks too much about uninteresting things
- **conservative:** sb. who refuses to accept change in traditional values
- **diehard:** sb. who fights new ideas and change
- **fogey:** sb. who is boring and old-fashioned
- **fossil:** sb. who belongs to a world that has become extinct because their old-fashioned views do not fit modern times
- **stick-in-the-mud:** sb. very earnest and maybe humourless who categorically refuses new ideas or trying new things
- **Neanderthal:** sb. who denies that modern ideas and things carry value

The 1950s

The 1950s were characterized by the beginning of the Cold War era, a growth of prosperity among the average population in the expanding suburbs, and radical changes in American society.

1. The USA had become the largest military superpower

The United States emerged as a world superpower after their victorious intervention in WWII. The nation's perception throughout the world had been transformed. In the years immediately after World War II, the United States dominated global affairs wanting to maintain democratic structures they had defended at tremendous cost and offering to share the benefits of prosperity as widely as possible.

2. The Cold War Period set in

After WWII western nations feared that the Soviet Union (then the USSR) would permanently dominate Eastern Europe and even infiltrate Western democracies. The tension arising between the United States and the Soviet Union became known as the Cold War and lasted for much of the second half of the 20th century. US American foreign policies sought to contain communism by diplomacy, threats or force. A series of international incidents occurred, such as in October 1962, the when the US and USSR came to the brink of a nuclear war during the Cuban Missile Crisis.

3. The nation enjoyed a booming economy

WWII was followed by a sustained period of economic growth which was accompanied by a surge in population. The government's effective combination of low taxing, balanced budgets and generous public spending on the construction of interstate highways, schools, the distribution of veterans' benefits and most of all the increase in military spending and the investment into new technologies such as computers contributed to the fact that the average US American population experienced a higher standard of living than ever before.

4. Suburbia and consumerism flourished

In the 1950s many middle-class Americans enjoyed more leisure and income than generations before them and so could define 'good life' in economic terms: cars, television, a home in the suburbs. Much of this consumer spending was done on credit with the newly introduced system of credit cards. Whereas population growth slowed in cities and decreased in rural areas, living on the outskirts of town became popular. From these rapidly growing suburbs people commuted to work, making the automobile more important than ever before.

5. The civil rights movement was on the rise

The NAACP (National Association for the Advancement of Colored People) as the leading civil rights organization in the US continually attacked the "separate but equal" rule by bringing cases to the courts to prove that separate facilities did not meet the equality criterion. In the Brown vs. Board of Education case the plaintiffs were thirteen parents on behalf of their 20 children. The daughter of one of the plaintiffs, Linda Brown, had to walk six blocks to her school bus stop to ride to an elementary school one mile away while a white school was only seven blocks from her house.

In the landmark case of 1954, Brown vs. Board of Education, the Supreme Court declared that "separate educational facilities" for black children were "inherently unequal" and thus unconstitutional. Consequently, implementation guidelines for how to desegregate schools were issued but it would take another 35 years until school integration reached its peak with 45 % of black students in the United States attending majority-white institutions.

6. Senator McCarthy led a crusade against communism

Some historians consider Senator Joseph McCarthy to be one of the least qualified, most corrupt politicians of his time. When a wave of fanatic terror against communism swept across the United States after WWII and at the beginning of the Cold War, McCarthy took advantage of this hysteria and started his campaign by presenting a list of 205 people in the State Department who were known members of the American Communist Party. A Senate committee was founded to investigate into the lives of private citizens, government officials, actors and others – among them Albert Einstein, who publicly condemned capitalism. Under McCarthy's order the Federal Bureau of Investigation kept a file with almost 1,500 pages of information on Einstein's allegedly subversive political activities.

Find out about some more facts of the 1950s at:
- http://www.history.com/topics/korean-war/videos/1950s
- http://www.thepeoplehistory.com/1950s.html

1. Match the illustrations above to the following social and political aspects.

2. With a partner discuss which of these aspects are incorporated in the movie to illustrate Walt's personality.

© Westermann Gruppe
Best.-Nr. 041295

The Korean War

1. Read the text and highlight five pieces of information that are of interest.
   Compare with a partner and agree.

2. With your partner discuss the information in the text to find arguments which support this quote:
   "The Korean war has always been an unpopular war among the American people." (Paul Robeson, American singer and civil rights activist)

   https://www.brainyquote.com/quotes/quotes/p/paulrobeso326896.html?src=t_korean_war [10.04.18]

After Korea had been occupied by Japan for thirty-five years, the country was liberated by the Allies after World War II. Its division into Communist North Korea under the in-
5 fluence of the Soviet Union, and an anti-communist South Korea under the influence of the United States left the region in a constant state of civil war.

In June 1950, North Korean armies moved
10 south across the 38th parallel, the dividing line, in an invasion of South Korea and provoked an international conflict. The Truman administration seeing North Korea's invasion as a challenge to the "Free World"
15 and the Soviet Union as an immediate threat to US American safety asked the United Nations for authorization to intervene.

As the US Congress never issued a declaration of war, this intervention was seen as "police action", which saw UN forces with nearly two million Americans serving push North Korea and its Chinese ally back beyond the
20 38th parallel and further north in a mission to re-unify the country by fighting back the forces of communism. This effort failed.

In the war which lasted three years from 1950 to 1953 at least 4.5 million people lost their lives – the vast majority of them Korean civilians and also 37,000 US American soldiers. Very cold winters, hot summers, steep slopes and ridgelines made serving in Korea extremely challenging. The US pursued a "scorched earth" policy
25 dropping Napalm bombs until the fighting lapsed into patrolling and controlling small local clashes and armistice negotiations began. The fighting finally ended in July 1953 and the front line has been accepted ever since as the boundary between North and South Korea.

The war has sometimes been called the 'Forgotten War' because within a few months most Americans, grow-
30 ing tired of a war that the US was not winning and so ignoring the conflict raging so far way, turned back to their own lives. Korean War veterans, most of them serious and patriotic men recognizing the failure of the war effort, came home exhausted, disillusioned and sometimes traumatized and tried to forget their wartime experiences to pick up their lives in the contradictory US mentality of the 1950s.

> For further information also see:
> - https://www.britannica.com/event/Korean-War
> - Howard Zinn. *A People's History of the United States: 1492 – Present.* Abingdon: Routledge, 2003.

original contribution by Ulrike Klein; photo: American Photo Archive/Alamy Stock Foto

---

[1] **napalm** a flammable liquid used against buildings and later against the population, causing severe burns

Hold at all costs

Hold at all costs. = Remain in your position or die trying with no possibility of retreat.

Discuss with a partner which of the quotes below most effectively reflects
- human bravery   ● the cruelty of war   ● the absurdity of war

a) "It seems remarkable after living for nearly a year under moment-by-moment dangers, how easily we conditioned ourselves to this abnormal way of living. This acquired conditioning created difficulties to become a civilian again. Peace and quiet without constant dangers makes re-entering civilian life seemingly unnatural[.]" Sylvester Poltorak, Korean War veteran

Erica Perdue: Korean War veteran, 82, shares poetry about his experiences, 28 May 2012, http://www.mlive.com/news/saginaw/index.ssf/2012/05/korean_war_veteran_82_shares_p.html [30.04.2018]

Outpost Harry was a remote US station on a hilltop during the Korean War. In a 9-day struggle heavily outnumbered American and Greek soldiers held their ground under massive artillery and mortar fire and in close combat in the trenches surrounding the station. Today it is considered "one of the decisive moments" in the Korean War. *Hold at all Costs* is the title of a Korean War Documentary about the battle of Outpost Harry. Korean War veterans from both sides recollect their memories of this battle.

b) "They said we don't expect you to come back from this patrol."
c) "He said this is a 'hold-at-all-costs situation'."
d) "He said, if anybody tried to leave, he would personally shoot us hisself."
e) "We went on Outpost Harry, we were walking on bodies for almost a mile up on the hill."
f) "The enemy penetrated our barbed wire. The order was wherever you saw shadows – you fire."
g) "The Chinese were pouring in over the trench line into the trench. I was just firing automatic, just dead center. They were 5, 10 yards from me."
h) "It took me a second or two before I shot one but then, once you get started at it, you're just like a rabid dog."
i) "Fire, fire, fire, fire. If you got artillery, you better be shooting."
j) "Then someone set that Napalm off and it set those Chinese on fire."
k) "You see it burning and you wonder how can anything survive. Two hours later they're cropping out of holes like rats coming at you."
l) "An American soldier grabbed me from the back, I grabbed his gun. I shot him dead."
m) "On the first night of the US fight I'd fired over 100,000 high-explosive rounds."
n) "This looked like one gigantic 4th of July fireworks display."
o) "No words can adequately describe the noise, the dirt, the screams."
p) "It was like mind-playing on you. How many times can you shoot and how many can you kill to psychologically break you down?"
q) "We love our comrades. We love the flag. We love our country. But it's not that exciting to say you held at all costs when you were the cost."
r) "A hero isn't someone in a spandex suit and a cape. A hero is a person who puts themself at risk for the benefit of another whether that other is next to them on the battlefield or a generation that hasn't even been born yet."

Quotes transcribed from: *Hold At All Costs: The Story of the Battle of Outpost Harry,* KPBS San Diego, California, USA, 2010, http://holdatallcosts.org; video on youtube: 12 November 2010: https://www.youtube.com/watch?v=8vAkK8oRiaA [30.04.2018]

This is not Korea

Walt's experience in Korea has shaped him to a great deal. The following scenes reveal what he lived through and how he deals with these memories:

☐ **scene 8:** Hanging out with the guys

☐ **scene 12:** Get off my lawn

☐ **scene 14:** Persisting

☐ **scene 41:** Preparations

1. Watch the scenes and match them with the appropriate analysis from the box. There are two more analyses than you actually need.

a)	During the war Walt has realized that life and death are inextricably interwoven, that they cannot be learned 'second hand' but must be experienced.
b)	Walt's war experience has taught him not to see the human in the one he killed and so the act of killing has in return dehumanized himself.
c)	In the war Walt learned to trust only in himself, to take things into his own hands and not to bank on anyone else.
d)	Walt believes he overstepped the bounds of duty during the war and therefore is lost forever.
e)	Walt has found a way to redemption and to reconcile the fate of the youth he killed in Vietnam with his own death.
f)	Walt is ready to sacrifice his life for Thao and his sister in the hope that he can thereby finally make amends for his shameful deed in Korea.
g)	Walt believes he lacks the strength other men showed and thus failed during the war.
h)	Walt is convinced the Christian faith lies about life and death.

2. When watching the scenes, also assess Walt's tone of voice and behaviour in the various situations. Now discuss with a partner what this says about how Walt has processed his war experience.

Granger Historical Picture Archive/Alamy Stock Photo

An American infantryman comforted by a comrade upon learning of the death of a friend in battle, 1950.

Thao: What it takes to be a man

Thao Vang Lor ist neben Walt Kowalski die zweite Hauptfigur des Filmes. Wie Walt durchläuft er eine tiefgreifende Veränderung und die Entwicklungen in beiden sind eng miteinander verwoben. Mit hängenden Schultern, den Blick gesenkt, wenig geachtet in der Familie und hin und her geschubst von der Gang seines Cousins, scheint Thao zu Beginn prädestiniert, das Schicksal junger Hmongs zu illustrieren, die ohne Halt zwischen zwei Kulturen in Gewalt und Kriminalität aufgerieben werden. Doch sein Gang-Initiationsritual schlägt fehl. Thao – durch seine Mutter und Schwester zu Wiedergutmachung gezwungen – findet in Walt einen fordernden und unnachgiebigen Mentor, der seine Stärken erkennt und fördert, ihn Leistungsbereitschaft, Verantwortung und Selbstachtung lehrt und ihn so in die traditionellen Werte Amerikas einführt.

Ziel der Arbeit mit diesem *Component* ist es, dass die Schülerinnen und Schüler zunächst Thao und seine Situation zu Beginn des Filmes einschätzen, die Herausforderungen begreifen, die ihm als *second-generation immigrant* entgegenstehen und abschließend seine Fortentwicklung beschreiben, indem sie reflektieren, welche Faktoren hierfür günstig sind.

Wie bereits für Walt Kowalski entwickeln die Schülerinnen und Schüler selbstständig und individuell auch für Thao ein *character portrait* (*Copy 15: Character frame*). Der Vergleich der beiden Porträts wird in der Arbeit in *Component 4* herangezogen.

3.1 Pacific by nature

In dem verunglimpfenden Namen ‚Toad' drückt sich in den ersten Szenen Walt Kowalski Verachtung für den Jungen von nebenan aus, später dann wird sich in diese Bezeichnung Zuneigung und Respekt mischen. Thao selbst weiß nicht wirklich wohin mit sich selbst. Wie das Klischee es will, ist er gut in Mathematik und steckt auch sonst gerne seinen Kopf in Bücher. Für die weiterführende Schule reicht das Geld der Familie aber nicht, und so steckt er fest. Er kann es niemandem Recht machen, den Frauen seiner Familie ist er nicht männlich genug, die Jungs in Spiders Gang wollen ihn mit Gewalt umerziehen, Walt verärgert seine Antriebslosigkeit und sein mangelndes Selbstbewusstsein. Der Druck dieser Außenwelt auf ihn zeigt Wirkung, er muss sich bewegen.

Da der Film sehr deutlich von der Figur des Walt Kowalski dominiert wird, muss der Fokus zuerst bewusst auf Thao gelegt werden. Dies geschieht zunächst mit einer kurzen Reflektion seines Namens.

> If you look up the name T(h)ao, the following explanations can be found: in Vietnamese, where it is most often used as a girl's name, it stands for honor and *respectful of parents*. In Chinese the name alludes to long life. In the Chinese philosophical tradition *tao* stands for *the harmony of yin and yang*, of complementary elements like shadow and light. Which of these symbolic meanings fits best for Thao, the Hmong adolescent in the movie? Explain your view.

 Ein kurzer Wortwechsel zwischen Walt und Thao (00:52:43) aus der Mitte des Films greift die Namenssymbolik auf. Walt verunglimpft Thaos Namen, Toad lässt an den Frosch denken, der zum Prinzen wird: "[Walt] [...] I knew you were a dipshit even before the whole garage deal, but I have to say you're even worse with women than you are stealing cars, Toad." – "[Tao:] It's Tao, not Toad. My name is Tao."

> In Walt's approach to Thao there are actually two insults.
> Why does Thao only react to the second?
>
> **Possible solution:**
> The first probably only confirms how Thao feels about himself, with the second Thao is offended that Walt gets his name wrong and he is not prepared to drop that issue.
>
> What do we as viewers make of Thao? Let us look at the events of that summer from his perspective.

In einem ersten Analyseschritt rekonstruieren die Schülerinnen und Schüler im *Think-Pair-Share*-Verfahren und mithilfe von *Copy 1* die Ereignisse des Films aus Thaos Perspektive. Im Plenum erläutern die Schülerinnen und Schüler kurz im Anschluss, welche möglichen Veränderungen dieser Perspektivwechsel mit sich bringen würde.

> How would the movie change if it showed Thao's view of things?
> Give three examples of scenes which would have to be added, changed or left out.

In Gruppen werden die Informationen zu Thaos Person verdichtet. Dies geschieht durch ein gelenktes Brainstorming in Form einer placemat, in die die Schülerinnen und Schüler spontan ihre Eindrücke von Thao in Rubriken wie *Things he likes, Things he hates, His most difficult challenges, His greatest achievement* niederschreiben, weiterreichen und ergänzen bzw. verändern. Im Zentrum vervollständigen sie dann gemeinsam für ihre Gruppe den Satz

The world needs Thao because ...

> Who is Thao Vang Lor? Enter your ideas into this placemat and present your version of the central sentence in class illustrating it with moments from the movie that you recall.
>
> **Possible solution:**
> For example: He likes books, maths, his sister, Wa Xam; he hates his situation at home, working in the garden or doing the dishes; his most difficult challenge is to defend himself against the gang, stand up against people who bully him, find his place; his greatest achievement is to overcome his fears and inhibitions and stand up for himself

Die spontanen Erinnerungen und Einschätzungen werden nun in einem Vergleich zwischen Walt und Thao bewertet, indem beide an den Eigenschaften eines traditionellen Leinwandhelden gemessen werden.

> Which of the two characters, Walt or Thao, is the more suitable hero for the screen? Remember movie heroes need to be virtuous, self-sacrificing, determined and focused, compassionate, persevering, dedicated to their cause, honest, loyal and responsible.
> Let us compare Walt and Thao on these grounds.

Possible solution to task 2 on *Copy 1*:

The movie probably favours Walt because his change is more radical; Thao is an adolescent who must find his way first; Walt has lived with his guilt for so long, his inner turmoil must be greater, his self-sacrifice in the end is obviously more dramatic.

Auch wenn Walt als Held im Zentrum des Geschehens steht, zeigt der Film dennoch, dass auch die Figur von Thao von Beginn an komplex angelegt ist und seine Eigenschaften besondere sind, sodass er neben Walt nicht nur bestehen kann, sondern ihn auch in mancher Hinsicht überragt.

Not only Walt may be the movie's hero, but Thao, too, learns to stand his ground. Although Walt considered Thao a coward and good-for-nothing in the beginning he calls him his friend and his equal in the end. Which qualities has Walt discovered in Thao?

 Anhand von vier Filmszenen analysieren die Schülerinnen und Schüler zunächst Thaos Verhalten mithilfe von *Copy 24*. Im Vergleich der Szenen erkennen sie abschließend grundlegende Haltungen, die diesen Charakter prägen sowie die Auswirkungen des Drucks, der auf ihm lastet.

Whereas Walt comes across in these scenes as his usual opinionated, pushy self, Thao displays many positive qualities. Take turns in naming and illustrating them.

Possible solution:
sensitive and kind, good-natured, honest, loyal, reliable and trustworthy, forbearing, morally upright

But all this does not seem to be enough. Thao is under pressure and makes a momentous decision when agreeing to steal Walt's Gran Torino. Where does the pressure come from?

Possible solution:
From his family who want and need a man in the house who takes responsibility and takes care of them, eventually also through a well-paid job. From inside himself because he is unhappy in the situation he is in, pushed around and mocked by his family, teased by Spider and his gang without any role model to look up to. From society which will only reward him a job and standing if he is educated, but college is too expensive.

Zum Abschluss dieser Sequenz und Vorbereitung auf die kommende fassen die Schülerinnen und Schüler ihre Erkenntnisse zu Thao in einem kreativen Schreibauftrag zusammen:

"My helpless brother"

 In a chat with a friend Sue expresses her worries about Thao. Praising his intelligence and qualities she also sees his ineffectiveness and lack of self-confidence. She wonders how he can be kept on track and not suffer the same fate as so many other Hmong boys.

3.2 At the crossroads

Thaos Frustration resultiert primär aus seiner komplexen Situation zuhause. Eine Familie ohne Vater und damit ohne Mann im Haus, drei Frauen, die Thao in Hmong Tradition erziehen: eine bittere, herrische Großmutter, eine wortgewandte und weitgehend amerikanisierte ältere Schwester, eine eher blasse Mutter, die die Auseinandersetzung mit dem amerikanischen Nachbarn scheut. Thao übernimmt widerwillig aber gehorsam in der Familie traditionelle Aufgaben von Frauen, den Abwasch oder die Gartenarbeit während das Haus ohne nennenswertes wirtschaftliches Einkommen verfällt und die Familie Sorgen um die Zukunft plagen. An den spirituellen Riten seiner Kultur hat Thao eher wenig Interesse, sein akademisches Können und Wissen versickert ungenutzt im Alltag. Dass es Zeit für Veränderung ist, weiß er selbst, aber er kennt den Weg aus der Sackgasse nicht.

Der Einstieg in diese Sequenz gelingt über die zuvor erzielten Schreibprodukte. In einer Redaktionskonferenz (3er-Gruppen) sammeln die Schülerinnen und Schüler unter der Überschrift *Thao's dilemma* aus den verschiedenen Produkten (*chat messages*, s.o.) Belege und einigen sich auf drei Hauptaspekte.

> Go through your writing and filter out indications which show that Thao finds himself in a dilemma. Agree on the three most convincing ones and present them to the class.
>
> **Possible solutions:**
> - He hates the household chores but has nothing better to do. He is helpful and willing but needs constant pushing. He is clever and intelligent but cannot go to college because it is too expensive. He has appropriate moral principles but lacks orientation in how to live them. He despises his cousin but cannot avoid him.
> - The people around him see his dilemma. They all want him to change, but each for different reasons.

Mithilfe der *Copy 25* (Task 1) erarbeiten die Schülerinnen und Schüler auf der Basis von Filmzitaten die Erwartungshaltung, die die Großmutter, die Gang und Walt an Thao stellen. Es zeigt sich, dass alle drei typisch maskuline Züge an ihm vermissen.

> **Possible solutions:**
> All these people complain that Thao lacks typically manly qualities: a masculine outer appearance, traits such as assertiveness, self-respect and self-confidence which help him to show his superiority over women, an interest in what is considered 'a man's job'. They want him to fit into their plans and schemes: the grandmother is interested in him managing and financing their household, the gang want him to subordinate to them instead of to his mother and sister, Walt would like to see Thao strive for American values such as self-reliance and personal freedom.

Da Thao zu allem schweigt, ersetzen die Schülerinnen und Schüler nun seine Stimme. In Kleingruppen entwickeln sie Antworten bzw. verbale Reaktionen auf drei ausgewählte Aussagen. Die Aussagen können an der Tafel notiert werden und die Ideen der Schülerinnen und Schüler in Form von Sprechblasen ergänzt werden. Wenn Zeit und Spielfreude der Gruppe gegeben sind, können diese Reaktionen auch als Stimmenskulptur ausagiert werden. Ziel wäre es hier, sowohl Thaos Gefühle zu inszenieren als auch mögliche Reaktionen der *bullies* zu antizipieren.

Lend Thao your voice and answer back.

1. "[Phong]: Look at him in the kitchen, washing dishes like a woman."
2. "[Walt]: You have no teeth. That's your problem. You have no balls."
3. "[Smokie]: [...] everyone thinks you're a pushover, [...] everybody walks all over you."

Thao weiß, dass alle Recht und Unrecht zugleich haben. Auch wenn er sicherlich aufgrund seiner kulturellen Prägung mit der Sicht seiner Großmutter übereinstimmt, erhält er von seiner Familie keinerlei Hilfe, wenn es um das ‚Wie' einer Änderung der Situation geht. Walt gehört noch nicht zu seiner Welt und so bleibt allein die Gang seines Cousins als mögliche Orientierung. Zweimal versuchen sie ihn auf ihre Seite zu ziehen. Der zweite Versuch glückt. Die Schülerinnen und Schüler analysieren die Gründe hierfür mithilfe von Task 2, *Copy 25*.

It is obvious that Thao is fed up with people nagging him. But there is nobody around to help him out of his dilemma. So, when Spider and his gang revisit he gives in to their bullying. Find out how they succeed.

Possible solutions:
use cool slang and buddy talk, encourage with their experience, display authority, insist on their solidarity and closeness, provoke with stereotypes

Spider and Smokie's tactics on the one hand surely have their effect on Thao, but how much would you say his wish to be 'part of something' weighs in on the other hand?

Das ständige Anecken macht einsam. So ist die Aussicht von der Gang protegiert zu werden auch die Aussicht auf bislang nicht gekannte Kameradschaft, ein gemeinsames Band. Aber allzu bald erkennt Thao, wie hoch der Preis hierfür wäre.

When Walt surprises Thao during his initiation ritual in the garage and threatens him with his rifle, Thao storms out and away from Spider and the others with the words 'I'm out!'. Paraphrase this shout to show what Thao turns against when he turns against the gang.

Possible solutions:
He turns against a cycle of violence, against leaving his own principles of what is right and wrong, against lowering himself to the level of his bullies, ...

Der Versuch aus seiner Misere auszubrechen ist zunächst gescheitert. Aber seine Tat hat für ihn ungeahnt positive Konsequenzen, denn seine Mutter und Schwester drängen auf Wiedergutmachung und bringen somit Walt Kowalski auf den Plan. Seine Qualitäten als Mentor werden sich auszahlen. Zunächst werden die Eigenschaften eines guten Mentors in einem Brainstorming zusammengetragen oder durch ein *ranking* der Lösungsvorschläge in den Fokus genommen.

Thao's first breakout has failed but it has also sharpened his senses. So what Thao actually needs is a mentor – someone to show him a way out of his misery and not add to it by making more claims on him. What other qualities must a mentor ideally have?

Possible solutions:

A good mentor …

- takes a personal interest without wanting something in return
- tries to develop a person's own strengths by exploring their attributes and be-liefs
- helps to set goals and give guidance in how to reach them
- is willing to share his knowledge and skills
- uses his communication skills to give positive feedback
- acts as a role model and motivates others by setting a good example
- values the opinions and initiative of others

Nun kann Walt an diesen Kriterien gemessen und der Erfolg seiner Steuerung von Thaos Ver-änderung bewertet werden. Es wird deutlich, dass Walt nicht alle Kriterien voll erfüllt, sondern Thao seine Stärken (*cleverness, natural skills, solid morals, continuous forbearing*) selbsttätig miteinbringen muss, damit der Prozess positiv verläuft.

- Apply the criteria to Walt and find examples from the movie on how he goes about teaching Thao about life.
- At the end of the summer Thao has thus learned a lot about himself and has acquired many useful skills which may help him in the future. With a partner create a list of the five top qualities you now see in Thao and five skills he has acquired.

Possible solutions:

Through Walt, Thao learns …

- how to make repairs on houses
- how to use tools
- how to respect himself
- how to behave as an American working-class male
- that he should look people in the eye, in contrast to Hmong cultural traditions
- the appropriate behavior for getting a job in construction
- not to become or be like Walt

and has become …

- self-confident
- optimistic
- dedicated
- assertive
- forceful
- more extroverted

Unter Walts wachsamem Auge lernt Thao viel über sich selbst und erwirbt verschiedene Fer-tigkeiten, die ihm am Ende einen Job einbringen. Um zu zeigen, dass sie Thaos Fortentwicklung auch aus seiner Sicht einschätzen können, schreiben die Schülerinnen und Schüler zum Ab-schluss dieser Sequenz einen *motivational letter* aus Thaos Perspektive unter der Verwendung einiger *prompts*.

Letter of Motivation: Thao Vang Lor

Applying for a scholarship for studying at a technical university Thao writes a letter of motivation in which he includes his qualities and skills. Start like this and make use of the prompts given.

Applicant for admission to the Civil Engineering program at Detroit University
Dear Sir or Madam,
I am currently … . Since my focus has increasingly centered on …, I would like to … .
What I can contribute to the program, in addition to my great enthusiasm for the field,
is … . I worked as … . … gave me hands-on experience and an increased understanding
of … Furthermore, I was able to … .
I am … person and an enthusiastic participant in … . I have … .
I appreciate you considering my application and I would be honored to be part of your
program.
Sincerely,

3.3 Riding off into the sunset

In dieser Unterrichtssequenz analysieren die Schülerinnen und Schüler, wie es Thao gelingt, sich aus seiner Unsicherheit zu befreien und durch seine Weiterentwicklung die Chance zu erhalten, in Amerikas multikultureller Gesellschaft seinen Platz zu finden.

Im Einstieg sind die Schülerinnen und Schüler aufgefordert zu beschreiben, welche Faktoren sich positiv auf die Weiterentwicklung eines jungen Menschen auswirken und welche Konsequenzen dies für ein förderliches Verhalten von Eltern hat.

Die folgende Übersicht mit möglichen Ansätzen hilft, die Aufgabe im Unterricht zu inszenieren: Im Partnergespräch *ranken* die Schülerinnen und Schüler zunächst die Angaben in der linken Spalte und diskutieren dann, wie sich die Faktoren (links) auf das Erlangen sozialer Fertigkeiten (rechts) auswirken und welche Rolle dabei das Verhalten von Eltern spielt.

- Which of the following factors do you consider most important for a young person's well-being and development?
- Taking turns explain how these factors relate to the challenges young adults face when growing up.
- Discuss how a parent's behaviour can influence this process.

People need to feel		be able to
☐ accepted		☐ assume responsibility
☐ challenged		☐ develop their own skills
☐ encouraged		☐ gain control over their lives
☐ fed and taken care of		
☐ free		☐ take on decision-making
☐ loved	in order to	
☐ noticed		☐ trust their own judgment
☐ nurtured		
☐ protected		☐ …
☐ respected		
☐ safe		
☐ supported		
☐ …		

Possible solutions:
Parents should …
- show their affection openly
- meet their children's physical requirements (food, clothing, healthcare …)

- be clear about their concerns but open to trust
- transfer responsibility but still support
- show interest in their children but not impose themselves
- be responsive when needed even if it is inconvenient
- refrain from harsh criticism or imposing their will

In einem nächsten Schritt, visuell stimuliert durch zwei Filmstills (*Thao washing dishes* vs. *Thao riding the Gran Torino* am Ende des Films), wenden die Schülerinnen und Schüler im *Lend-me-your-eyes*-Verfahren die Faktoren und sozialen Fertigkeiten auf Thao an und bewerten ihn damit in der jeweiligen Situation.

- Judging Thao in the scene given explain which of the expressions can be applied to him.
- What has changed that makes Thao more confident at the end of the film?

Mit der Frage nach dem Unterschied in den Einschätzungen zu Beginn und am Ende des Films ergibt sich auch die Frage nach den Verantwortlichkeiten und dem Einfluss der Umgebung auf Thaos Entwicklung.

Zunächst soll nun hier die allgemeine Situation der jugendlichen Hmong, so wie sie im Film angesprochen ist, deutlich gemacht werden (*Copy 12*). Dies geschieht über den Vergleich einer kurzen Filmszene (1:09:26 – 1:10:30) mit dem Script. Die im Film ausgelassenen Passagen des Scripts geben Aufschluss über Herausforderungen in den Bereichen Rollenverständnis, Bildungschancen und Kriminalität.

Die Schülerinnen und Schüler gehen also folgendem Impuls nach:

- What is the general situation young Hmongs are confronted with in the US?
- Which differences can be seen according to gender?

Die Ergebnisse dieses Arbeitsschrittes können wie folgt zusammengefasst werden:

Invisible boys

Challenges in growing up: How to	Hmong girls	Hmong boys
• live between two cultures	slip in and out of cultures more easily are able to keep a foot on each side of the fence	[are lost]
• cope with new freedoms in the US	date who they want	
• find moral guidance	stay close to their mothers	need fathers, but the fathers belong in a totally different world, they cannot give advice to their sons
• master the educational system	go to college	[drop out of school, join gangs]
• succeed in life		end up banding together and it all goes to hell from there go to jail
	→ adapt more easily	→ fall through the cracks, float around

Am Ende des Films scheint Thao vor einem typischen Schicksal gerettet. Die Antwort auf die Frage nach dem ‚Wie kam es dazu?' soll nun mithilfe einiger Szenen erarbeitet werden.

> Let us understand which people and circumstances in Thao's life have contributed to the fact that he has grown into a confident young man at the end of the film.

Nachdem die Schülerinnen und Schüler relevante Momente im Film situiert haben (*Copy 26*), erarbeiten sie in Gruppen (insofern sie mit mobilen Endgeräten arbeiten können) die Etappen auf Thaos Weg und präsentieren diese im *gallery walk/one-stays-three-stray*-Verfahren. Sie entwickeln hierfür in der Analyse der einzelnen Szenen einen *freeze frame*, nehmen dabei Thaos jeweiligen Gemütszustand in den Fokus, um im Vergleich eine Entwicklung deuten zu können. Hilfestellungen zum Thema *body language* finden sie auf *Copy 27*.

> - Watch the scene closely and observe Thao's verbal and non-verbal reaction. Transfer the crucial moment of the scene into a freeze frame which to you expresses Thao's state of mind best. In your group discuss the message Thao's body language conveys.
> - Present your freeze frame to the class, illustrating your choice with aspects from the movie.
> - Let us align the different illustrations with more general stages of human transformation processes. (*Copy 26*, task 2)

Possible answers:
1. **Resting stage:** Eggs are laid on the leaves, they are tiny and hard to find.
   Thao's potential is there (good-hearted, kind, helpful, empathetic) but not yet appreciated. He feels invisible, pushed around, like he is not enough and does not know enough. Yet, he knows there must be something bigger to come.
2. **Growth stage:** The caterpillar eats, grows and expands.
   Thao wants out and tries his options with the gang, but must then 'feed' on Walt's influence.
3. **Transformation stage:** Metamorphosis goes on unnoticed from the outside – the caterpillar changes its shape and form.
   Thao has found a mentor who supports his growth and protects him from all negative influences so that Thao can focus. He realizes what he is capable of and asserts himself.
4. **Leap stage:** The butterfly emerges from the chrysalis and learns to fly.
   Thao must cope with setbacks but stays focused. He has learned that he has to do it on his own, make his decisions and take responsibility. To be called 'a friend' by Walt is the final recognition, an honor.
5. **Productivity stage:** The caterpillar reproduces.
   Thao might use all that he has learned and experienced so far to master new challenges and/or to help others.

Thaos Entwicklung zeigt, dass sich Selbstvertrauen und Sicherheit in Wechselwirkung von eigener Anstrengung und Bestätigung von außen entfalten. In Ergänzung zu diesen menschlichen Qualitäten, die Thao nun gefestigt hat, galt das Interesse seines Mentors Walt auch dem Ausbilden typisch männlicher Qualitäten. Diese sollen nun abschließend noch einmal betrachtet werden. Hierfür *brainstormen* bzw. *ranken* die Schülerinnen und Schüler zunächst einmal Eigenschaften, die Männlichkeit beschreiben.

> Now that Thao has risen to his potential as a human being, the question remains if Walt has also succeeded in strengthening Thao's male characteristics.

Rank the given traits to show what Walt considers masculine attributes and apply them to Thao.

A real man …

- ☐ admits when he made a mistake
- ☐ avoids anything 'girlie'
- ☐ can fix things
- ☐ cares about his physique and his appearance.
- ☐ defines himself by possessions like a fast car or a big home
- ☐ has gentleman qualities
- ☐ has strong opinions and defends them
- ☐ holds himself accountable.
- ☐ is firm in his conviction
- ☐ is himself without apologizing for it
- ☐ keeps his body in shape
- ☐ keeps a gun in his home
- ☐ knows how to assert himself
- ☐ knows what he wants
- ☐ learns from his failures
- ☐ puts others before himself
- ☐ serves as a role model to others
- ☐ …

Um diesen im Film für Thao gezeigten Prozess zum Ende zu führen, schließt die Phase mit einem kreativen Schreibauftrag ab, in dem die Schülerinnen und Schüler Thao diese Phase seines Lebens und die Rolle von Walt rückblickend betrachten lassen:

Back then

Ten years later Thao returns to the old neighborhood and recollects what happened. Walking through the streets he remembers Walt and pays tribute to him. Create an interior monologue which reveals both how Thao's life has continued and what he feels Walt has contributed to his life of today.

Appearances can be deceiving

In Walt's eyes Thao is hopeless, weak-willed and has no self-respect or dignity.
The following excerpts from the movie show why Walt changes his mind.

The girls go to college, the boys go to jail. (scene 17, 00:37:37)

1. Watch the scene, match the actors' body language accordingly and add their effect: e. g. genuine interest, irony, doubt, only assuming, giving a lecture, wanting to bring the message home, …

"[WALT:] But what about that dimwit brother of yours?

a) eyes interlocked

_____
_____
_____

He a little slow or something?"

b) casually glancing sideways towards the other

_____
_____

"[SUE:] Tao is actually really bright,

c) focusing on the other squinting, lips pursed

_____
_____
_____

he just doesn't know which direction to go in."

d) eyes wander off

_____
_____
_____

"[WALT:] Oh, poor Toad."

e) looking ahead deliberately accentuating the words

_____
_____
_____

"[SUE:] It's really common. Hmong girls over here fit in better, we adjust. The girls go to college, the boys go to jail."

f) showing a quizzical expression

_____
_____
_____

Explain Sue's worries about her brother and speculate on the effect this scene has on Walt.

Look at that (scene 18, 00:39:16 – 00:40:10)

2. Watch the scene and finish the sentences according to your understanding.

a) The scene shows …
b) Walt's comment "What the hell is it with kids nowadays?" shows that in general he expects young people to …
c) When Thao appears, Walt's comment "How about that, Daisy?" expresses his …
d) His disgusted grunt is aimed at … because …

Now explain in one sentence what Walt recognizes on Thao's behalf here.

© Westermann Gruppe
Best.-Nr. 041295

Count the clouds (00:57:04 – 00:57:48)

3. Bring the dialogue back into its correct order. Then watch the scene and discuss with a partner which of the three expressions best fits Thao's state of mind: humiliation – exasperation – anger.

☐ "[**WALT:**] Yeah, of course you pay. You have no teeth, you have no balls, kid."

☐ "[**TAO:**] Go ahead. I don't care if you insult me or say racist things. Cause you know what? I'll take it."

☐ "[**WALT:**] Because unlike you I'm not useless. I maintain my property. You swamp rats, on the other hand, you just can't help it ..."

☐ "[**TAO:**] So, what do you have for me today? You want me to watch paint dry, maybe even count the clouds that pass by?"

☐ "[**WALT:**] Don't get flip with me, boy. I'm not the one who tried to steal, don't you forget that."

☐ "[**TAO:**] Look, I'm stuck here. Why don't you just find something useful for me to do?"

Bringing up the freezer

4. Label the speech bubbles with either **Walt** or **Thao** to show who says what. Comparing this dialogue to the one above, name three differences which show that Thao's change to a more self-confident young man also shows in the language he uses.

"I just need a little push. All the weight is up top, so you stay down and give me a little shove at each step."
_____

"Let me take the top."
_____

"Naw, I got it."
_____

"No really, I'll take the top. It looks pretty heavy."
_____

"Look, I'm not crippled. I got it."
_____

"If you don't let me take the top, I ain't helping. I'll go back home."
_____

"Now, listen to me, zipper head..."
_____

"You listen, old man. You came and got me because you needed help, so let me help you. Either it's top or I'm out of here."
_____

"Okay then, be my guest. Just don't let it slip out of your little girl hands and crush me."
_____

"Don't give me any ideas."
_____

Flying solo

1. The following sentences and expressions all refer to Thao. Sort them into categories showing who uttered them, **Phong**, **Walt** or **Spider** or a member of his gang. Paraphrase the meaning of what they say and find words and expressions to show what they expect of Thao, how they want him to be.

☐ "[…] everyone thinks you're a pushover, […] everybody walks all over you"

☐ "[H]e flies solo"

☐ "[H]e's got nowhere to go."

☐ "Even his sister gives him orders and he obeys."

☐ "Good luck, puss-cake. You need it."

☐ "He a little slow or something?"

☐ "Hey, moron."

☐ "I mean, look at you, out here working in the garden like a woman."

☐ "I own you."

☐ "I used to be kind of a quiet little punk like you, everybody fucking with me."

☐ "If we all stick together, shit like that won't happen."

☐ "Look at him in the kitchen, washing dishes like a woman."

☐ "Thao's not a man."

☐ "That old woman's got bigger balls than you."

☐ "This kid doesn't have a chance."

☐ "We have to man you up a bit."

☐ "You can't be such a little girl."

☐ "You have no teeth. That's your problem. You have no balls."

☐ "You just need a little guidance."

☐ "you're a big fat pussy!"

2. Spider and Smokie bully Thao into joining their gang (00:15:40 – 00:17:30). Analyse their tactics. Here are some key phrases:

> "Hey, you wanna roll with us now?"/"Come on, ride with us."/"You need somebody protecting you, right?"/"I've been there, I've done it and I've seen it."/"Back in the day, everybody wanted to beat me up but nobody wants to fuck with me now."/"Come on, man, let's go."/"We're cousins, right? We're family."/"A brother to Spider is a brother to me."/"Shed that, that's a woman's work, man."

3. **Plans for life (scene 30, 01:10:31 – 01:13:01):** Watch the scene and compare Walt's mentoring skills to the gang's bullying. Name three differences to explain why Walt's training proves successful in the end.

© Westermann Gruppe
Best.-Nr. 041295

A long way

In the movie Thao undergoes a thorough change. The following scenes reconsider the different stages of this process.

1. Situate the quotes into the context of the film by matching them to the correct scenes.

Quotes | Scenes (Thao)

1
"[SMOKIE:] That's exactly the point, Tao. Spider told me how everyone thinks you're a pushover, how everybody walks all over you and shit. I mean, look at you, out here working in the garden like a woman."

a) talked into stealing the Gran Torino by Spider's gang

b) confronted by Spider's gang on his way home from work

2
"[WALT:] That's about what I expected. Okay, why don't you go over by the spruce tree and count how many birds feed at the bird feeder?"

c) at the reading of Walt's testament

3
"[TAO:] You listen, old man. You came and got me because you needed help, so let me help you. Either it's top or I'm out of here."

d) on his first day of work for Walt

e) helping Walt to carry up the freezer

4
"[TAO:] The Gran Torino? You'd let me drive it?"
"[WALT:] Sure. Why not."
"[TAO:] Really?"
"[WALT:] Really."

f) watching Walt repair the faucet in Thao's home

g) at Walt's for a barbecue

h) after washing the Gran Torino

5
"[TAO:] No. Don't let me down, Walt. Not you. This is going to end, today."

i) over at Walt's house the day after the attack on Sue

6
"[WALT:] You've come a long way. I'm proud to call you a friend."

j) locked in the basement by Walt

2. In psychology, human growth is often compared to the five stages of the butterfly transformation process:
   1. **Resting stage:** Eggs are laid on the leaves, they are tiny and hard to find.
   2. **Growth stage:** The caterpillar eats, grows and expands.
   3. **Transformation stage:** Metamorphosis goes on unnoticed from the outside – the caterpillar changes its shape and form.
   4. **Leap stage:** The butterfly emerges from the chrysalis and learns to fly.
   5. **Productivity stage:** The caterpillar reproduces.

   Discuss with a partner whether this can be applied to Thao and his change. Illustrate the different stages with his experience.

Body language

To understand what people actually say when they are not saying anything it helps to decode their body language. Here are some examples.

EYES	people probably
looking right (generally)	make things up, fabricate 'alternative facts', guess, lie
looking left (generally)	state or retrieve 'facts' from memory, remember things
direct eye contact	are honest, pay attention
widening eyes	demonstrate their interest in the matter
rubbing the eyes	show disbelief, are upset, or tired
shrugging the eyes	reveal their frustration
blinking frequently	are excited, under pressure
winking	express friendly acknowledgement, complicity (e.g., sharing a secret or joke)

MOUTH	
pasted smile	fake it
tight-lipped smile	are secretive, withhold their spontaneous reaction and emotions
twisted smile	show mixed feelings or sarcasm
bottom lip jutting out	are upset, seek sympathy
laughter	are relaxed
forced laughter	are nervous, in need of empathy
biting a lip	are tense
teeth grinding	anxiously suppress a natural reaction
pursing lips	show thoughtfulness or are upset
hand clamped over mouth	hold back, are shocked
nail biting	are frustrated or afraid

HEAD	
slow head nodding	listen attentively
head held high, chin jutting	display their superiority, fearlessness, arrogance
head tilted to one side	are thoughtful, feel submissive
chin up	show their pride, defiance, confidence

ARMS	
crossed arms (folded arms)	are defensive, reluctant
arms held behind body with hands clasped	show confidence, authority
seated, holding drink on one side with hand from other side	show nervousness

SHOULDERS	
raised, head lowered	are tense, nervous, anxious, fear an attack
hunched, arms folded	are afraid, under pressure
curved forward	feel defensive, threatened, do not want to be seen
pushed back, chest forced out	demonstrate power and dominance
shrug	say 'I don't know'

Illustrations:
© Leremy/fotolia.com

© Westermann Gruppe
Best.-Nr. 041295

HANDS

palm(s) up or open	pretend to be innocent, show their submission, appeal to the other
palm(s) down	display their authority, strength, dominance
hand(s) on heart	seek to be believed
finger pointing (at a person)	are aggressive, threaten
finger wagging (side to side)	give a warning, refuse the other person something
hand chop	emphasize their words
clenched fist(s)	want to resist, show aggression and determination
thumb(s) up	give positive approval, agree, signal that all is well
thumbs down	show their disapproval, failure
rubbing hands together	show anticipation, relish
ear tugging	are undecided
hands clasping head	are shocked
hand stroking chin	express thoughtfulness
neck scratching	are doubtful, show disbelief
running hands through hair	are vexed, exasperated
hand(s) on hip(s)	are self-confident, ready to attack
hands in pockets	show disinterest, feel bored
handshake	demonstrate dominance with the 'upper hand', submission with the 'lower hand'
handshake – equal and vertical	are relaxed
pumping handshake	are enthusiastic

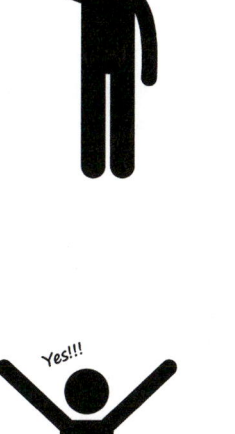

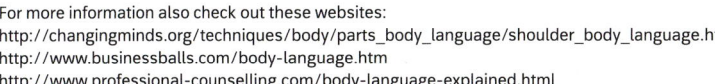

For more information also check out these websites:
http://changingminds.org/techniques/body/parts_body_language/shoulder_body_language.htm
http://www.businessballs.com/body-language.htm
http://www.professional-counselling.com/body-language-explained.html

Illustrations:
© Leremy/fotolia.com

© Westermann Gruppe
Best.-Nr. 041295

Separate but unequal: Life in modern suburbia

My neighbourhood – in dem Film erheben alle Bewohner den alleinigen Anspruch auf ein und dasselbe Viertel einer amerikanischen Großstadt: Walt Kowalski, der die Gegend in ihrem Verfall kaum mehr wiedererkennt, seine Widersacherin Phong Lor, die nicht verstehen kann, warum er als einer der wenigen Weißen noch hier ist, Thao und Sue, ihre Enkel, für die es Heimat ist, ein junger Latino, der mit seiner Gang der asiatischen Gang die Herrschaft über die Straße abtrotzen möchte. Sie alle leben hier in *separate communities*, und wenn sich ihre Wege kreuzen, dann sprechen Ablehnung und Gewalt. Menschen mit höherem Einkommen zieht es in die äußeren *suburbs*, wo sie unbehelligt von Bauruinen und Bandenkriminalität ihr Leben genießen. Im Film kennt nur Walt eine andere Realität, die Vergangenheit, in der Menschen wie er, weitgehend Familien der Arbeiter aus den Ford-Werken, hier ihr Vorstadtleben bescheiden und ehrlich – man könnte auch sagen bieder und konformistisch – lebten. Die Zeiten haben sich geändert, die Geschichte und Identität Amerikas hat Menschen aus anderen Kulturen hierher gebracht, und nun stellt sich die Frage, ob und wie sich ein Zusammenleben gestalten lässt. Engstirnigkeit und Vorurteile auf beiden Seiten ziehen Grenzen zwischen Nachbarn, Institutionen versagen, und kriminelle Gangs haben diesen Teil der Vorstadt übernommen. Der Film setzt sich mit zwei Einzelschicksalen auseinander und spielt doch meist mit den Klischees einer multikulturellen amerikanischen Gesellschaft. Walt ist Traditionalist, durch den Krieg gebrochen beharrt er umso mehr auf den typischen amerikanischen Werten von Freiheit und Eigenständigkeit und lebt sein Recht auf Waffenbesitz. Die Kirche, der er angehört, ist schon lange nicht mehr seine spirituelle Heimat. Die Lor-Familie hält ebenfalls an ihren Traditionen fest, die in der neuen Heimat exotisch anmuten. Gleichermaßen muss die junge Generation anders als die alte ihren Weg in das Amerika des 21. Jahrhunderts finden. Auch hier entzieht sich der junge männliche Vertreter den spirituellen Gebräuchen seiner ethnischen Wurzeln. In beiden Kulturen bedeutet dies einen Verlust, der erst am Ende durch die Verständigung auf gemeinsame ethische Werte, ein gemeinsames Verständnis von *richtig* und *falsch*, kompensiert werden kann. Ob hierin auch der Lösungsansatz für das Zusammenleben in multikulturellen Gesellschaften allgemein liegt, beantwortet der Film vorsichtig positiv.

Dieses *Component* bietet Fragestellungen an, die vom Film aufgeworfen werden und der individuellen Beantwortung durch den Zuschauer bedürfen. Es geht hier insbesondere um Fragestellungen der Zugehörigkeit.

In einem ersten Teil betrachten die Schülerinnen und Schüler die Bedeutung familiärer Beziehungen in solchen *separated communities*, bevor sie ihren Blickwinkel weiten und gesellschaftliche Realitäten in den Blick nehmen, die Individuen ebenfalls ein Gefühl der Gemeinsamkeiten und der Zugehörigkeit vermitteln können. Am Ende dieser Unterrichtssequenz steht dann die Frage nach Überwindung von Grenzen und Abschottung im Zentrum und die Schülerinnen und Schüler analysieren die Antworten, die der Film und seine Protagonisten bereithalten.

4.1 Your porch or mine?

Das Bild von Walt und Phong auf ihren respektiven Veranden prägt sich ein. Bei Walt ist sie solide, aus Stein, er liest dort Zeitung, trinkt sein Feierabendbier und blickt mit seinem Hund Daisy auf die Welt, die er nicht mehr versteht. Phong sitzt in ihrem Schaukelstuhl auf einer maroden Holzveranda, strickt und kaut Betelnüsse. Kreuzen sich ihre Blicke, so wird geschimpft, gefaucht und gespuckt. Die beiden alten Menschen in dem Film sind die Verkörperung der kulturellen Identitäten. In ihren Häusern wird dem Tod und dem Leben gedacht, Vertreter von Kirche und Religion gehen ein und aus, Kinder nennen es ihr Zuhause.

Während Walt nach dem Tode seiner Frau am liebsten ungestört und alleine seinen Alltagsbeschäftigungen nachgeht, herrscht nebenan stets rege Betriebsamkeit, Familie und Freunde gehen ein und aus; Walt empfindet Father Janovich als Irritation, der Schamane nebenan ist Mitglied der Familie und von allen geachtet. In beiden Familien gibt es Zwietracht, aber auch den Wunsch nach Nähe. Betrachtet man ihre Einrichtungen, so sind sie sich erstaunlich ähnlich, einfach, solide, unauffällig. Diese Unterschiede und Gemeinsamkeiten sollen in einem ersten Schritt thematisiert werden.

Den Schülerinnen und Schülern wird zum Einstieg in zwei Gruppen jeweils ein still von Walt und von Phong auf der Veranda gezeigt (scene 11, 00:23:13; scene 20, 00:42:12).

> Study how Walt and Phong fling accusations at one another. Which substantial problem do they have with one another? What do they base their judgment on? Despite the obvious contempt, work out nuances of truths in their words.

Im Anschluss werden sie gebeten, Themen für *small talk* mit den beiden zu vorzuschlagen.

> Imagine you were visiting these two old people at their home. What would you talk about with them? (For example about their children, their home, what they have done during the day, how they feel, compliment them on the flowers and plants they keep ...)

Im Folgeschritt werden in Partnerarbeit die Antworten der beiden zu den angesprochenen Themen formuliert und in der Gruppe verglichen. Im Plenum werden diese Antworten in Beschreibungen der beiden Figuren überführt und ein Vergleich eingefordert.

> Let us collect and compare the information we get on these two characters, for example:

	Walt	Phong
family situation	a widower two sons, four grandchildren	a widow lives with one daughter and two grandchildren in the same house
home	a house in the suburbs with a front and back yard	a house in the suburbs with a front and back yard
daily routines	maintaining the house spending some time on the porch	looking after the family spending some time on the porch
worries	• misses his wife • feels estranged from his insensitive and greedy sons and their families • his neighbours are all foreigners who do not belong here and let their house fall into disrepair	• misses a man in the house • her grandson has not turned out the way she hoped • her nephew's gang is threatening her grandson • the white man next door does not really belong here anymore

Der Vergleich ergibt, dass sich beide Figuren in ihrem Alltag sehr ähnlich sind. Beide würden dies allerdings vehement bestreiten und einander beschuldigen, der jeweilige Eindringling im gewohnten Umfeld zu sein. Die Schülerinnen und Schüler betrachten zunächst in arbeitsteiliger Einzelarbeit (*Think-Pair-Share*, aufsteigende Gruppen) die von beiden geäußerte Antipathie genauer und vergleichen dann ihre Ergebnisse.

> Even if their lives and worries compare, Walt and Phong fight like cat and dog whenever their paths cross. What do they hold against each other? Compare their tirades of hate.

Possible solutions:
Their antagonism is not based on a particularly bad experience in the past. There has not been a problem so far. On the contrary they do not know each other at all but judge each other by appearance. Walt hates all Asian-looking people from the start. Obviously Walt is traumatized by his experience in Korea which may explain but not apologize for his disdain for Asian people. He accuses Phong and her family of not maintaining their property, which is true, but he ignores the fact that they lack a man with the necessary skills or money to do so. Phong is right in saying that the area is an all-Asian neighbourhood except for Walt. This however is not a privilege she can demand. She also shows her superstition, believing men like Walt bring bad luck. The viewer will not remember her words but that rather the entire circumstances in the neighbourhood and not Walt personally are responsible for the attack on Sue.

Im Plenum werden diese Ergebnisse vertieft, indem die Begrifflichkeiten *stereotype, prejudice, racist behaviour* mit den Äußerungen von Walt und Phong in Verbindung gesetzt werden.

> So, if Walt and Phong have never met, what are their comments about the other based upon? Explain the words *stereotype, prejudice, racist behaviour* in this context.

Possible solutions:
Both Walt and Phong have a stereotypical view of the other (e.g., all American white males bring bad luck, all Asians do not maintain their property) which lets them use slurs and mutter insults. As long as they do not act upon their words or hurt each other they only nourish their prejudices about the other culture but are not yet openly racist in their behavior.

Vor allem in der Sprache zeigen sich hier also rassistische Vorurteile. Nun spricht Phong nicht Englisch, ihre Präsenz im Film ist auf wenige Szenen limitiert, und deshalb werden in der Folge Walts Äußerungen in den Fokus gerückt, um die Frage zu beantworten, wie verletzend Sprache sein kann.

> - Maybe we can smile at Walt and Phong's feud. Throughout the film, however, we hear Walt use derogatory terms for people he sees in his neighbourhood. This overuse of unseemly language raises the doubt whether Walt is not, after all, a racist in contempt of all other cultures than his own. Before we have a closer look at his language, let us test our sensitivity of politically correct language.
> - Based upon what you already know from English classes, comment on the appropriate use of the words: African Americans, Afro-Americans, blacks, Negroes, the N-word.

Copy 28 erläutert den Begriff *racial slur* sowie die Funktionen, die eine solche Sprache im Kontext übernimmt und listet verschiedene rassistische Bemerkungen auf, die Walt im Verlauf des

Filmes zu seiner Sprache macht. Die Schülerinnen und Schüler werden durch Task 2 aufgefordert, herauszufinden, welche möglichen Intentionen hinter den einzelnen *slurs* zu vermuten sind. Durch das *Think-Pair-Share*-Verfahren erarbeiten sie die Ergebnisse zunächst in Stillarbeit, bevor sie mit dem Partner und dann im Plenum diskutiert werden.

> To understand the motivation behind Walt's racial slurs we must analyse them in the context he uses them and understand what in particular fuels his contempt for Asian Americans.
>
> **Possible solutions** *(Copy 28)*:
> The analysis of Walt's slurs shows that they are a consistent part of his language. His conscious overuse of expressions of disdain and contempt against Asian-looking people who remind him of the enemy in Korea makes him use racial slurs to express camaraderie with friends as well when unconsciously overreacting because he is insecure.
> Walt's bias against Asian Americans is fueled by …
> - his traumatic experiences in Korea
> - the fact that Asians in his neighbourhood live in neglected-looking houses and have 'strange' customs
> - the fact that the invasion of Asian cars has ruined the American auto industry in which Walt worked for so long

Die Intention des Filmes scheint also, die Frage offenzulassen, ob Walts Äußerungen ihn zu einem Rassisten machen. Dies soll Gegenstand der abschließenden Schreibproduktion sein. Vorab werden die Schülerinnen und Schüler deshalb zu einer anderen Bewertung aufgefordert. Bevor Thao in Walts Vorstellung von einer Männerwelt bestehen kann, muss auch er eine andere Sprache lernen.

> Now that we have seen that Walt's use of racial slurs serves different functions let us turn to the scene where Thao must learn to 'optimize' his language to become a man.

Die Schülerinnen und Schüler analysieren zunächst die respektive Filmszene mithilfe von *Copy 13* und bewerten dann Walts Ziele.

> According to Walt, what should the language Thao uses convey?
>
> **Possible solutions:**
> Through his words and his posture Thao must assert himself and show that he is in control of the situation. When he talks 'like men talk' he can prove he is one of them and they will respect him.

Thao gelingt es auf diese Weise, einen Job auf dem Bau zu bekommen. Insofern war Walts *tutorial* erfolgreich. Ob *slurs* allerdings tatsächlich einen wertvollen Beitrag für Thaos Leben bringen, soll der abschließende Schreibauftrag evaluieren.

Words do matter

> Even if Thao has landed a job with his new language skills, the question remains of what value these skills will prove in the future and whether they are an appropriate means of finding his way into American society.
> Elaborate your view on the effects of racial slurs promoted by Walt as acceptable by expanding on one of the following comments.

1. Talking like a man means trading racist insults. This is a lesson Thao does not need.
2. It is a flaw in the script of *Gran Torino* that all of Walt's relationships with peers are based on a shared exchange of overtly racist language.
3. The movie should be rated R (R = Restricted, children under 17 require an accompanying adult) because it overuses racial slurs and very often plays them for laughs.
4. *Gran Torino* is a problematic movie. The use of racial slurs adds to the fact that all the Hmong characters in the film are either weak and in need of protection or they are depraved criminals.

4.2 Moving in, moving out

Sprache ist auch eine Möglichkeit der Identifikation für die Mitglieder der verschiedenen Gangs, die im Film das Bild der Vorstadt prägen und ihre Bewohner drangsalieren. Latino und Asian Gangs kontrollieren die Straßen, schwarze Jugendliche lungern herum, provozieren. Jeder reklamiert sein Territorium, Waffen sind neben Beschimpfungen Mittel der Auseinandersetzung. Als Nebenprodukt verschiedener Einwanderungswellen bieten die ethnisch orientierten Gangs den Jugendlichen der *second generation* eine zweifelhafte Zuflucht, die häufig durch Diskriminierung, Herkunft aus benachteiligten Familien, Marginalisierung ihrer Wohngebiete ihren Platz in der *mainstream society* vergebens suchen. Auch der Film nimmt dieses Konzept auf und zeigt Delinquenz und Gewalt als Folge von Verarmung und Ausgrenzung. Die in den 1950er-Jahren neu entstandenen *suburbs* sind durch Verwahrlosung grau geworden, und die Mehrheit der weißen Amerikaner, die sie einst aufbauten, bzw. deren Kinder, ziehen weiter in neu entstehende Wohngebiete außerhalb, in denen luxuriös eingerichtete Eigenheime, gepflegte Rasenflächen vor dem Haus und Swimmingpools im Garten Wohlstand spiegeln und in denen Menschen leben, die es sich leisten können, Situation in den Innenbezirken zu meiden und zu ignorieren.

In diesem Abschnitt erkennen die Schülerinnen und Schüler in der Realität der Straßengangs die Folge von nicht funktionierender Integration(spolitik) und setzen sich damit auseinander, wie Individuen mit dieser Realität umgehen.

Dazu sehen sie sich in Anknüpfung an die vorangegangene Sequenz zunächst mit Filmzitaten (*Copy 29*) konfrontiert, die sie in ihren Kontext einordnen sollen und an denen sie typische Merkmale eines Soziolektes wahrnehmen können.

- We have been talking about Walt's language. Let us continue down this path to understand the function language can take in shaping our impression of a person. Take a look at the following quotes (*Copy 29*). Who could have said them, and in which context?
- Can you make out any difference between the language Walt uses and the slang used by the different gang members?

Es wird deutlich, dass sich Walts Sprache auch den Verhältnissen in seinem Viertel angepasst hat und er sich auf diese Weise – und natürlich auch mit seinen Waffen – Respekt verschaffen kann.

One can see that Walt can communicate effectively with the different gangs and groups in his neighbourhood and therefore overcome the dangerous situation. The movie shows two different gangs roaming the streets of Walt's neighbourhood. How realistically does the movie depict gang culture and the threat for citizens like Walt?

Mit Task 3 der *Copy 29* sowie einem Zusatztext (*Copy 30*) lesen sich die Schülerinnen und Schüler zunächst Wissen an, das es ihnen ermöglicht, die Darstellung im Film realistischer einzuschätzen und benennen dann die Gefahren, die von diesen Banden ausgehen.

- Explain how Spider's gang in particular impacts the lives of the ordinary people in Walt's neighbourhood.
- How do the people react? How do Walt's sons see the problem? And what about Walt?

Das Treiben der Gangs scheint ihn mehr zu ärgern als zu stören. Neben seiner Abgeklärtheit und seiner Wortgewandtheit ist Walt meist bewaffnet unterwegs.

Possible solution:
In contrast to the Asian community in this part of town, who hide in their houses, and Walt's sons who have moved out of this part of town and live in false security and ignorance, Walt cannot be intimidated and actively confronts the gang. His age, his illness, and his war experience seem to make him immune to fear. His effective language helps him to resist.

Bereits auf dem *movie cover* ist Walt mit Gewehr abgebildet. Aus dem Krieg hat er sich ein Gewehr aufbewahrt, Messer und Revolver gehören auch zu seiner Sammlung. Sein Freund Martin hat ebenfalls ein Gewehr in seinem Salon. Sie setzen dem Unrecht etwas entgegen, lassen sich nicht einschüchtern.

What else commands the respect of the gangs? Walt keeps several guns in his house and in his car. Do you think self-defence for living in a dangerous neighbourhood is the main reason for this?

Possible solutions:
In the US there is the constitutional right to own and bear guns. Walt is one of many. The fact that he actually draws on his guns, however, is maybe more exceptional. He even brought one of his rifles home from Korea, where the use of a gun regulated the soldiers' lives. It seems as if using his guns is the only way Walt has learnt to solve a conflict, especially one with members of a foreign culture. Having killed so many men in Korea, people may lose their humanity behind a gun sight. So Walt can focus on the problem, on the wrong and right of things.

Diese Reflexion wirft zumindest Zweifel daran auf, wie berechtigt Walts Waffeneinsatz ist. Um dies genauer zu überdenken, treten die Schülerinnen und Schüler in Partnerarbeit in einen vom Lehrer gesteuerten *Brainstorming*-Prozess (S.C.A.M.P.E.R.) ein, indem sie auf die ihnen gestellten Fragen Antworten finden.

How do you feel about Walt's relationship to guns? Let us have a look at what the alternatives would be. Make sure to discuss them in the frame and the logic the movie offers.
Let us take the situation in which Walt gets Sue out of trouble.
- What would have happened in the scene if Walt did not have a gun on him? (Substitute)
- How would the gang members have reacted if Walt had continued talking with his forefinger stretched out and thumb cocked? (Combine)
- What would have been different if the situation had happened downtown; let us say in front of the barber's? (Adapt)

91

- Who else on the spot could have done something to de-escalate the situation? (Modify)
- What led to the aggravation of the situation in the first place? How could this have been avoided? (Eliminate)
- What would have to change so that a situation like that does not happen at all? (Reverse)

Possible solutions:
It is difficult to say which alternative could be effective in this situation because the movie does not offer any. The area in which the gang members have a go at Sue is desolate. There is nobody around, above all no police patrol car. The black youths immediately address Walt when he gets out of his truck. There are three of them and they are physically stronger.

In der Tat kann es nur schwer gelingen, diese konkrete Situation aufzulösen. Deshalb wird die Problematik auf eine abstraktere Ebene gehoben und die Gewaltspirale angesprochen, die Walt an anderer Stelle auslöst.

Even though the lack of obvious alternatives may justify Walt's reaction here, his constant insistence on pointing a gun at anyone who comes in his way and using violent force to put an end to a conflict, however, does not go without consequences in the movie.
The saying *violence begets violence* (echoed in Phong's words that "a man like him brings nothing but sorrow and death") seems to hold true in the movie.

Mithilfe von *Copy 14* füllen die Schülerinnen und Schüler individuell die Gewaltspirale und vergleichen ihre Logik mit der von Walt, der die Verantwortung alleine bei Spider und seiner Gang zu sehen scheint und deshalb seinen letzten Vergeltungsschlag plant, der der Gewalt im Viertel ein Ende setzen soll.

Who does Walt hold responsible for what happened to Sue? Would you agree considering the spiral of violence you created?

Possible solutions:
Contrary to Walt who puts all the blame on the gang, the viewer can see Walt's part in the situation, too. Walt's forceful intervention in his front yard and when he was revenging Thao has escalated the bloodlust of the gang. Knowing that Thao and Sue have a strong protector in Walt, they time their perfidious assault well when they know that Walt is not around.
Walt plans to put an end to this violence by sacrificing his own life against all pleadings by Father Janovich not to seek retaliation. The viewers in the end have to decide for themselves whether this will change anything for the neighbourhood in the long run.

Am Abschluss dieser Sequenz steht eine *good-angel-bad-angel activity*, die einen Schreibauftrag vorbereitet. Die Schülerinnen und Schüler wägen ab, wie sinnhaft es ist, Walts Kampf zu kämpfen oder ob es nicht besser wäre, es seinen Söhnen gleich zu tun und das Viertel mit seinen Miseren hinter sich zu lassen.

Walt's life seems to have been dedicated to taking on the responsibility for his neighbourhood and the people in it whereas Walt's sons have decided differently.

They have left this neighbourhood behind and raise their families in a safer part of town where they can live their lives in peace.

If Thao reaches the age where he can freely decide what to do, stay or move out of this neighbourhood, what would you advise him to do?

- One half of the class prepares arguments for Thao to stay, the other for Thao to move out.
- When finished, form two groups mixing the viewpoints.
- Decide on one student in each group who takes Thao's role.
- Confront this student with the arguments and let him or her make an own decision.
- Both decisions will be presented to class and argued for by using the three main reasons.

Im Plenum werden die beiden Entscheidungen miteinander vergleichen und die Argumentationen ggf. durch Nachfragen vertieft. Im Anschluss wird der Schreibauftrag gegeben:

The right to own a gun

"People sleep peaceably in their beds at night only because rough men stand ready to do violence on their behalf." (George Orwell)

Relate this quote to the movie and comment on it.

4.3 Choose to love thy neighbour

In *Gran Torino* ist die Frage zentral, inwieweit *ethnicity* das Selbstverständnis eines Menschen prägt und seine Beziehungen zu anderen Menschen steuert. Die Schülerinnen und Schüler begegnen in diesem Film einer ihnen aller Voraussicht nach unbekannten kulturellen Identität. Thao Lor, der Junge aus Walts Nachbarhaus, ist Hmong. Das Schicksal dieser indigenen Volksgruppe Südostasiens, die heute in den Bergen von China, Laos oder auch Vietnam leben, führte mehr als 100 000 von ihnen in die USA, nachdem sie während des Vietnamkrieges an der Seite der US-amerikanischen Truppen gekämpft hatten. In den USA leben sie heute vor allem in den städtischen Ballungszentren von Kalifornien, Minnesota oder Michigan. Der Film thematisiert in prägnanter Weise wesentliche Aspekte, die den typischen Alltag von Hmong in den USA charakterisieren, so z. B. das Festhalten an Sprache und kulturellen Traditionen, mangelnde Orientierung und Integrationsprobleme junger Hmongs, *gang violence* oder auch Alltagsrassismus von Seiten der weißen Bevölkerung.

Die abschließende Unterrichtssequenz steht im Zeichen interkultureller Lernerfahrungen der Schülerinnen und Schüler. Am Beispiel der Kultur Hmong lernen sie Brückenschläge kennen, die helfen, Andersartigkeit als Chance zu erkennen.

Für den Einstieg wird der Screenshot, der Sue und Thao in Hmong-Tracht während des Trauergottesdienstes für Walt zeigt (1:45:18), ausgewählt.

Sue and Thao have come in their traditional costumes to mourn Walt. What might be their reasons?

Die individuellen Spekulationen der Schülerinnen und Schüler werden im Plenum gebündelt und in die Zielsetzung dieser Sequenz überführt:

Although we have been able to dive into Sue and Thao's lives for nearly two hours there is yet little that we know about their understanding of their culture and traditions.

Who in the film seems the most steadfast when it comes to understanding Hmong culture?

Um die Schülerinnen und Schülern in das Leben der Hmong im multikulturellen Amerika der Gegenwart einzuführen, wird zunächst die entsprechende Filmszene zu einer ersten Bestimmung des Begriffes Hmong genutzt (*Copy 9*).

- What does the viewer learn about the Hmong in this scene?
- Which common perceptions of white Americans do Walt's comments show?

Possible solutions:
Asia seems to be one country, not a continent. The climate of the American Midwest is not healthy for Asian people coming from tropic jungle areas.

- Comment on the way Sue lectures Walt here. What does this tell us about her experience as Hmong in the US?

Possible solutions:
She has heard similar comments before. She seems above it all and does not feel annoyed but rather challenged to set things right by clarifying and explaining things to people like Walt. She is not intimidated by racist comments, because she sees herself on par with Walt.

Im Anschluss an die Bearbeitung der Filmszene sollen Sues Erläuterungen in einen größeren Kontext eingebettet werden. Zu Beginn dieser Phase wird den Schülerinnen und Schülern zunächst noch folgende Aufgabe präsentiert.

Which of the following considerations would you include when describing your cultural identity?

> **shared history and fate, common geographic location and language, traditions and values, world views, social class, religion**
> **or rather**
> **dissociation from other ethnicities**

Die Schlüsselbegriffe können genutzt werden, um diese *Food-for-thought activity* methodisch in Szene zu setzen, z. B. in einem *Four Corners*, einem *Double Circle* oder auch einer *Placemat activity*. Im Vergleich zum Unterrichtsgespräch wären so alle Schülerinnen und Schüler aktiviert. Aus dieser vorbereitenden Aufgabe kann dann auch der Leitimpuls für die Lesephase abgeleitet werden:

Let us find out which aspects must be considered when describing Hmong identity.

Arbeitsteilig lesen die Schülerinnen und Schüler zwei Texte (*Copy 31* und *Copy 32*), die die Rolle der Hmong während des Vietnamkrieges einerseits und ihr Schicksal nach dem Ende des Krieges genauer beleuchten. Sie präsentieren ihre Ergebnisse im Plenum, die wie folgt in einem Tafelbild zusammengefasst werden können.

Hmong

- is the name of a farming people who in the past lived predominantly in the hills of Laos.
- the US recruited Hmong to fight on their side during the Vietnam War.
- Hmong civilians suffered bombarding and disease all through the war.
- considered enemies of the Laos state after the war, the Hmong were displaced and put into labor and refugee camps in Laos and Thailand.
- American authorities allowed educated Hmong to settle in the US.
- Their fate as a displaced people with no country to call home has shaped their identity and kept their culture alive.

Die Schülerinnen und Schüler wählen jeweils in 3er-Gruppen fünf Screenshots aus, die zeigen, wie der Film das Leben der Hmong in den USA darstellt. Im Prinzip der aufsteigenden Gruppen vergleichen sie ihre Auswahl untereinander und einigen sich am Ende auf eine gemeinsame Auswahl von fünf Illustrationen, die im Plenum kommentiert werden.

- Choose and agree on five screenshots which illustrate the life of Hmong as the film depicts it. What has changed for them in the US?
- Which reasons can be found to explain the Hmongs' obvious lack of integration into mainstream society? Who should intervene on an institutional level?

Hier wird nun bewusst die institutionelle Ebene angesprochen und der Film nur ggf. an den Stellen herangezogen, in denen sich Father Janovich offensichtlich verantwortlich fühlt, aber nicht viel ausrichten kann. Mit der Frage, wer für Integration Verantwortung tragen sollte, werden die Schülerinnen und Schüler aufgefordert, zunächst durch ein *food for thought* (*double circle, positioning line*, Punkteabfrage) staatliche Aufgaben zu überdenken und dann persönlich-individuelle Möglichkeiten zu erkennen.

How effective do you consider the following measures governments can take to promote integration?
- School should be the most effective tool for integration.
- Financial incentives should convince immigrants to learn the language.
- Cities should adapt their cultural facilities (museums, spiritual spaces, …) to the meet the needs of immigrants in their communities.
- Minorities should be discouraged from moving into and forming ethnic ghettos.
- States and communities should introduce sponsor programmes in which citizens introduce immigrants to the American values and life-style.
- As a nation born of immigrants the US and its government should make integration their top priority over foreign policies.

Auch in die individuelle Verantwortung des Einzelnen soll appelliert werden und die Schülerinnen und Schülern so auch an ihr eigenes Leben Fragen richten.

Obviously there are state responsibilities but there are probably also ways that private citizens can become involved. If we think of the film we can see that Walt overcomes his prejudice only late in his life and then he is surprised to see how much he has in common with the foreigners from next door.

> What can people like us do to prevent prejudice and welcome immigrants into our lives?

Die individuellen Ideen aus der Gruppe werden im Plenum gebündelt und ggf. vertieft.

- As many of your ideas show, it is important to get to know about the other, to open up to other cultures and understand and accept their way of living in the hope that they will do the same. This is best done through experience – like Walt. Only he puts his foot in with every step he sets into the Lor house, not knowing a thing about Hmong culture.
- In today's world there are many possibilities to become informed a little beforehand.

Im Folgenden entwickeln die Schülerinnen und Schüler einige nützliche Hinweise zur Kultur der Hmong.

> On the Internet, people post information about their culture to make others aware of what is dear to them and which cultural aspects they ask others to respect. Do some research on Hmong culture.
>
> Work out clues which also might have been helpful for Walt.

Nachdem diese Aufgabe gelöst wurde, soll ein ähnliches Produkt für die amerikanische Kultur entstehen, so, wie Walt sie im Film vertritt. Damit wird für diese Sequenz ein kreativer Abschluss gefunden, der beide Perspektiven vereint.

On US American life

> If Walt had to define US American culture and values and explain to his Hmong neighbours what he considers important for them to know to live a content life in the United States, what would he have said?
>
> Create a feature (text, pictures, music) and present it to class.

Words do hurt

The movie Gran Torino was heavily criticized for containing too many racial slurs. Were they gratuitously used or are they due to the circumstances and characters the movie presents?

1. To fully understand the upcoming quotes from the movie make yourself acquainted with the meaning of the unseemly expressions used by matching them with their explanation.
   Remember that all the terms here are derogatory slang and must not be used in conversation or in writing.

   a) zipperhead
   - a degrading term American soldiers frequently used for the enemy soldiers in the Korean War

   b) chink, fish head, egg roll
   - a pejorative term used for people of Asian origin; coined during the Korean War by frontline troops in allusion to soldiers that were run over by enemy troops in jeeps, leaving tire tracks on their bodies in a pattern resembling that of a closed zipper

   c) mick
   - a racist term to describe Chinese people;

   d) dago
   - a slur used for Korean people; distortion of the Korean word for Korea: "Hanguk"

   e) swamp rats
   - an ethnic slur for a person from Italy, Spain or Portugal

   f) spook
   - a derogatory term for a person of African descent

   g) dragon lady
   - a derogatory slur used for Vietnamese or Asian people in general, alluding to the slope of their eye

   h) slope
   - a slur for a manipulating and deceptive Asian woman

   i) gook
   - a derogatory term for Irish people

2. *Slurs* are derogatory expressions directed at an entire class of people, targeting these groups on the basis of race ("chink"), nationality ("paki"), religion ("kike"), gender ("ho"), sexual orientation ("dyke"), immigrant status ("wetback"), culinary preferences ("rice bag"), or others.
   Slurs …
   - are used to emphasize the speaker's attitude toward someone
   - express the speaker's current emotional state (e.g. anger, shock, insecurity)
   - denote an aggressive reaction to a specific person and their actions or words
   - express the speaker's sense of power and superiority
   - establish and reinforce group identity, "camaraderie", or male bonding

   Read the following quotes from the movie carefully, bring to mind the context they are used in and decide which of the above mentioned functions the racial slurs have in each instance.

   a) *Walt's comment when he sees people pouring into the neighboring house for the birth ritual:* "How many swamp rats can they cram into a room?"
      Walt to Thao when he comes to work for Walt: "I maintain my property, whereas you swamp rats let your houses go to hell."
      Walt to Smokie when he attacks him at his home: "Is that all you swamp rats or is there more vermin scurrying in the shadows?"

   b) *Walt when he shuts the door in Thao's face on the day of the funeral:* "And have some goddamned respect, zipperhead, we're mourning over here."
      Walt to Thao in the basement of the Lor home during the barbecue: "Relax, zipperhead, whatta you think I'm gonna do, shoot you?"

Dialogue between Walt and Thao about Thao getting a decent job: "Is that why I see you out in your garden all the time? Besides, zipperhead, we ain't in Hu-Mong." – "Funny."

Part of Walt's testament: "And don't put a big gay spoiler on the rear-end like you see on all the other zipperheads' cars."

c) *Walt's comment about his neighbors' garden:* "Damn chinks let their yards go to hell."

Walt's comment on passing the Silver Star to Thao: "In Korea, October, 1952. We were sent up to sweep a Chink machine gun nest that had carved us up pretty bad. I was the only one who came back… I received the Silver Star. I want you to have it."

d) *Comment of a Latino gang member attacking Spider:* "Why gooks come up in here and fuck up our neighborhood?"

Walt's comment to Father Janovich after the brawl on his lawn: "In Korea, we never 'called the police' when a swarm of screaming gooks came pouring into our lines. We reacted."

Walt's comment at the Lor barbecue after the Shaman read him: "I've got more in common with these goddamned gooks than my own spoiled-rotten family."

e) *Walt and the barber at the barber shop:* "I'm just amazed that you're still alive. I keep hoping you'll die and they'll get someone good in here, but you just hang in there, you dumb, Italian-Wop-Dago, you." – "That'll be ten dollars, Walt."

f) *Walt's question for the black guys threatening Sue:* "What makes you spooks think you can bully a couple kids with impunity?"

g) *Walt's comment after having touched a girl on the head at the Lor barbecue:* "What?! What the hell are all you fish heads looking at?!"

h) *Walt lectures Thao about Yao in the basement of the Lor home:* "Wrong, egg roll. I completely know what I'm talking about. I know I'm not always the most pleasant person to be around, but I got the greatest woman who ever lived to marry me. I had to work at it, but I got her and it was the best thing that ever happened to me. Hands down."

i) *Walt asks Thao on his first day of making amends:* "Yeah, you can count? You slopes are supposed to be good at math, right?"

j) *Sue and Walt talking on his porch:* "And you're a good man." – "Hand me a beer, Dragon Lady."

3. With a partner discuss possible triggers for Walt's particular bias against Asian-Americans.

© Westermann Gruppe
Best.-Nr. 041295

The lingo of the streets

The language of the streets. This is what slang is sometimes called. Influenced by different languages, dialects, cultures and sayings it knows many variations depending on the location, the speaker and the times. Gangs develop their own specific system of spoken language.

1. Here are some quotes from the movie. Can you identify the speaker and the situation and 'translate' their meaning into proper English?

   "You hard-nosed, Polack, son of a bitch."

   "It's all cool, bro."

   "What's wrong with this nigga?"

   "I didn't think your ass would've came."

   "Now, get your ofay, Paddy ass on down the road."

   "Oh good, more fucking rice niggers."

   "We'll catch you on the rebound, homey."

2. Inform yourself about some typical aspects of slang used by gangs. Illustrate some of these aspects with examples from above.

   a) Each gang can be identified by the specific slang they use.

   _____

   b) This slang has its own vocabulary, especially phrasal idioms which only the gang members can identify correctly. When conditions change, words will change.

   _____

   c) Sometimes words are borrowed from a foreign language.

   _____

   d) Many terms are ambivalent: derogatory when used for intimidation and aggression, affectionate when used among members.

   _____

   e) Fixed expressions work like a code to specify types of situations, locations, the enemy, ...

   _____

   f) Although words may sound or look familiar they may take on a different meaning. Or the other way round: established concepts may have new expressions when new words are coined.

   _____

   g) Sometimes sounds are distorted to imitate a dialect or other language.

   _____

   h) Sentences lack grammatical correctness and are usually kept short.

   _____

i) Imperatives are frequent.

_____

j) More emotional attitudes than facts are frequently expressed.

_____

3. **Now watch the following scenes:**

Rivals: 00:12:40 – 00:14:16
At the barber's: 00:29:44 – 00:30:22
All cool, bro: 00:30:22 – 00:34:47

Identify some of these common characteristics of gangs in the movie.

a) Members identify themselves through a name, symbols, hand signs, terminology, and beliefs.

_____

b) Neighbourhood-based gangs often perpetuate violence, drug distribution and other crimes.

_____

c) Gangs develop their own spoken language or terminology according to their needs, goals and activities.

_____

d) Rivalries between gangs are often based on race.

_____

e) Gangs usually have an exclusive territory (turf) and show street presence.

_____

f) All members of a gang exhibit a common culture.

_____

g) The culture of a gang is imparted from one generation to the next.

_____

h) Some gangs require potential members go through initiation ceremonies.

_____

i) The norms of a gang define which behaviours are expected and accepted among its members.

_____

j) Respect is a cherished value in most gangs.

_____

k) Gangs are usually organized and hierarchically structured.

_____

l) Gangs are often criminally active: rape, robbery, aggravated assault, gun crimes and murder are frequent.

_____

> For more information on US American gang culture and violence see:
> https://www.nationalgangcenter.gov/About/FAQ
> https://www.fbi.gov/file-repository/national-gang-report-2015.pdf/view

Out there on the streets

The FBI says that there are some 33,000 violent street gangs, motorcycle gangs, and prison gangs with about 1.4 million members criminally active in the US and Puerto Rico today. Their reports show that gangs continue to grow in numbers and expand their criminal activities.

Kiyo Dörrer: Gang crime in the United States – MS-13: The rise of a deadly gang in US suburbia

The last few years have seen a surge in violence by the notorious MS-13 streetgang in the US, especially in middle-class suburbs. But will President Trump's plan to arrest, jail and deport its members stop the violence?

At first glance, the towns of Montgomery County on the outskirts of Washington, DC seem like any other suburbs [...]. But this seemingly harmless region experienced 18 gang-related deaths in the last two years, with further possible cases currently under investigation. A majority of them were committed by the notorious MS-13 gang. [...]
5 The gang is best known for its brutal tactics. In one of Montgomery County's malls, a 16-year old ordered the killing of two teenagers, who were chased, stabbed and just barely managed to escape. Last summer, an 18-year old was lured into a park in the county and stabbed 153 times by gang members. Another 18-year old was also stabbed and then stoned while he tried to crawl away from his assailants. He was found dead
10 underneath a bridge. This type of brutal violence by young members of MS-13 is not just the problem of DC's suburbs: [...] similar cases have been reported nationwide.
On an official visit to Long Island in July, US President Donald Trump announced "to every gang member and criminal alien, we will find you, arrest you, we will jail you, and we will deport you." But the reality of fighting the recent spread of gang violence is, as
15 so often, more complicated than that. [...]
MS-13, also known as Mara Salvatrucha, is a street gang founded in the 1980s in Los Angeles by El Salvadorian undocumented immigrants. They spread to the East Coast in the 1990s, but are now active in 40 states in the US, as well as the "Northern Triangle" of Honduras, Guatemala and El Salvador.
20 The recent rise in gang violence in the US is attributed to a crackdown on gangs by the El Salvadorian government. Their strategy of the "mano dura," or "iron fist," has led to a loss of revenue for MS-13 in the country [...]. To compensate that loss, the gang has ramped up activities in the US. [...] Their brutality is part of their tactic to increase their standing and influence. "If I use a machete and hack your body up, it sends a message
25 that permeates through those communities," says Paul Liquorie, head of special investigations at the Montgomery County police. [...]
The police have made numerous arrests [...]. But the more widespread and subversive gang activities are the ones that are harder to combat. MS-13 mostly engages in extortion, human trafficking and drug dealing and was known to target illicit businesses such
30 as underground restaurants, bars or brothels. But in recent years, the activities have expanded to target members of the immigrant community who own legal businesses. Crimes like these are harder to fight against because the victims themselves are less likely to report to the police. "There is the fear of the gang and the reprisal of the gang and they are also skeptical of the law enforcement [...]," says Liquorie. "And then there
35 is the crackdown on illegal immigration by the current administration, which makes them less likely to come forward and to speak to authorities." [...]
Arrests alone also don't stop the growth of the gang. [...] Gang members of MS-13 ac-

tively target children as young as 12, registering some of themselves in school solely for the purpose of recruitment or buying ice cream for the children of a whole neighbor-
40 hood. "We know that it is particularly impacting unaccompanied children that are now in the school system," says Abel Nunez of CARECEN, an organization helping Central American immigrants. Having often experienced trauma in their home countries – sometimes at the hands of gangs as well – and being more prone to living in difficult family environments, they are seen as "low-hanging fruit." [...] [G]ang members ini-
45 tially seem to offer these children what they desperately need: a sense of belonging. If recruitment targets do not respond to this approach, MS-13 resorts to threatening the target's family back in their home countries in Central America, where American au-thorities cannot intervene. "The irony of that is also that many of the young people fled to the US with the hope of escaping the gangs," McCarthy adds. [...]
50 As to the "deport" part of Trump's strategy: "Deportation is a tactic, not a strategy," says Liquorie. "We have seen time and time again people who have been deported returning back to the United States because they are already networked into the criminal element that is running the human smuggling routes."
Instead, those on the ground agree that the most effective way is to try and offer alterna-
55 tive activities and safe spaces to those who are most vulnerable to recruitment. Mont-gomery's recreational department arranges soccer and after-school study groups to keep at-risk children out of the reach of the gangs. The education system also empha-sizes bringing those newcomers up to speed with extra classes to help them integrate faster into the surrounding community. [...] But the core problem of improving the fam-
60 ily environment to make the home a safe space away from gangs is the hardest to ac-complish – and not one solved either by ice cream or by deportation.

from: Deutsche Welle, 02 September 2017, http://www.dw.com/en/ms-13-the-rise-of-a-deadly-gang-in-us-suburbia/a-40321825 [03.05.2018]

1. Skim the text to see whether it confirms the FBI findings.

2. Scan the text for information which can be illustrated by scenes in *Gran Torino* and which helps to explain gang activity in the movie.

The Hmong and the war in Vietnam

For thousands of years, the Hmong have maintained a distinctive culture, including dress, oral literature and religion, valuing their autonomy and close-knit community above all. In pre-war Laos, the ethnic
5 identity of the Hmong remained intact, because they lived high in the mountains and had little contact with other people. They farmed in the highlands and harvested enough crops for their own needs. Opium was their only cash crop.
10 In the late 1960s, when the Vietnam War spread into Laos, the United States recruited the Hmong to fight against communism. Wanting to hold on to their land and the independence they had maintained for thousands of years, the Hmong saw communism as a
15 threat to their autonomy. Hmong soldiers, totaling over 30,000 men, fought the ground war, flew combat missions, directed air strikes, rescued downed American flyers, fought behind enemy lines, gathered intelligence on the movements of North Vietnamese
20 troops and more. They suffered heavy casualties for their brave involvement in the war: Hmong soldiers died at a rate ten times as high as that of American soldiers in Vietnam.

Before the war, between 300,000 and 400,000 Hmong
25 lived in Laos. Although there is disagreement over how many died during the war, estimates range from one tenth to half of the Hmong population was killed. Some were soldiers, but most of the dead were civilians felled by mortar fire, land mines, grenades, post-
30 war massacres, hunger and disease. One hundred and fifty thousand Hmong have fled Laos since their country fell to communist forces in 1975.

Displaced from their villages after the war, which were either bombed out or burned by the North Viet-
35 namese and the new Lao communist regime, many Hmong became refugees in their own country. U.S.-sponsored food drops – fifty tons of rice a day – fed more than 100,000 Hmong, whose land and livestock had been destroyed by the war.

In February 1973, the Vientiane Agreement was 40 signed, calling for a cease-fire in Laos, a coalition government and the end of U.S. air support. American relief programs ceased, and the Lao's People Party declared the Hmong enemies of the state. Between 1,000 and 3,000 Hmong, mostly high ranking army 45 officers and their families, were airlifted to Thailand, while thousands more who had fought for the CIA or remained neutral in the war were left behind. In a ravaged country strictly controlled by the North Vietnamese, many Hmong were forcibly relocated to 50 lowland areas and assigned to state-owned collective farms. More than 10,000 Lao intellectuals, civil servants, teachers, police officers and other suspected royalist sympathizers were interned in „seminar camps" for forced labor and political indoctrination. 55 Fearing retribution and famine, most chose to migrate to Thailand on foot, journeys on which many Hmong died from disease, starvation, exposure and drowning while crossing the Mekong River which borders Laos and Thailand. 60
Once in Thailand, most Hmong were placed in Ban Vinai camp on the Thai/Lao border in the northeast part of the country near the Mekong. The camp had no electricity, running water or sewage disposal, and was severely overcrowded. At its peak in 1986, Ban 65 Vinai had 42,858 residents, 90 percent of whom were Hmong. The Thai government closed Ban Vinai in 1992.

Because of their American military ties, many Hmong who left the refugee camps chose to come to the Unit- 70 ed States. The best educated Hmong and Lao were allowed entry into America first. The U.S. government gradually allowed more refugees as years passed. Around 200,000 Hmong currently live in the United States, most of whom reside in Minnesota, central 75 California and Wisconsin.

from: http://www.pbs.org/splithorn/story1.html [20.12.2017]
© PBS/Taggart Siegel/Collective Eye Films. The Split Horn: Life of a Hmong Shaman in Amerika

Identify 10 pieces of relevant information and use them to inform another student about the Hmong and the Vietnam War.

I am Hmong

1. Which of the following considerations would you include when describing your cultural identity?

> shared history and fate, common geographic location and language, traditions and values, world views, social class, religion
> or dissociation from other ethnicities

2. Now read the excerpt below to explain which elements this writer names to explain her cultural identity.

In Ban Vinai Refugee Camp, Loei Province, Thailand: December 1980 – January 1987

From the day that she was born, she was taught that she was Hmong by the adults around her. As a baby learning to talk, her mother and father often asked, "What are you?" and the right answer was always, "I am Hmong." It wasn't a name or a gender, it was a people. When she noticed that they lived in a place that felt like it had an invisible fence made of men with guns who spoke Thai and dressed in the colors of old, rotting leaves, she learned that Hmong meant contained. The first time she looked into the mirror and noticed her brown eyes, her dark hair, and the tinted yellow of her skin, she saw Hmong looking at her. Hmong that could fit in all of Asia, Hmong that was only skin deep.

In Phanat Nikhom Transition Camp to America,
Chonbur Province, Thailand:
January 1987 – July 1987

The feeling that she was Hmong did not happen until the preparations for America began as her family was being processed. Thailand wanted to close its refugee camps, send away the remnants from the war:
You are going to America on a one-way ticket.
You are going to America as refugees of the Vietnam War.
You are going to America as Hmong from the camps of Thailand.
You are going to America to find a new home.
We do not want you here anymore.
All this was said in the things that were happening: the classes that her mother and father attended that taught them new strings of words ("Hello. How are you? I am fine, thank you."); new kinds of food (piece of chicken between bread with cilantro and green onion and a white, tasteless, fatty spread from a jar); the free set of clothing that each person was given: a dark blue sweater, walking shoes with laces, white socks, dark blue pants, a white collared shirt to go underneath the sweater. These were the Thai government's last gift to the Hmong for leaving their country, the American government's donation to a people who had passed exams stating they had fought under American leadership and influence during the Secret War in Laos from 1960 to 1975. All this was felt as she watched the preoccupied adults around her preparing for a new life, trying to end the yearning for an old one that she didn't know – she saw how their eyes searched the distance for the shadows of mountains or the wide, open sky for the monsoons, one last time before it was gone forever.
All these good-byes made her feel very Hmong inside.

Kao Kalia Yang, excerpt and picture from *The Latehomecomer: A Hmong Family Memoir*. Copyright © 2008 by Kao Kalia Yang. Reprinted with the permission of The Permissions Company, Inc., on behalf of Coffee House Press, www.coffeehousepress.com

© Westermann Gruppe
Best.-Nr. 041295

Bildquellenverzeichnis

|alamy images, Abingdon/Oxfordshire: American Photo Archive 67; Classic Stock 66; Granger Historical Picture Archive 69 u.; Jeff Morgan 08 66; PhotoStock-Israel 66; Stocktrek Images, Inc. 66; Vintage Corner 66; WENN Ltd 35, 35; Wyn Williams, Gari Wyn 3; ZUMA Press, Inc. 35. |Domke, Franz-Josef, Hannover: 24, 24. |fotolia.com, New York: beermedia 33; leremy 84, 85, 85, 85, 85, 85, 85, 85, 85, 85, 85, 85, 85, 85. |Getty Images, München: FilmMagic/LaVeris, Jason 35; Rodriguez, Alberto E. 35, 35; Toronto Star/Stuparyk, Michael 35. |Kassing, Reinhild, Kassel: 26, 26, 26, 27, 27, 27. |stock.adobe.com, Dublin: Gabrieuskal 35. |The Permissions Company Inc., Mount Pocono: Kao Kalia Yang, excerpt from The Latehomecomer: A Hmong Family Memoir. Copyright © 2008 by Kao Kalia Yang. Reprinted with the permission of The Permissions Company, Inc., on behalf of Coffee House Press, www.coffeehousepress.com 104. |Warner Bros. Entertainment Inc., Burbank/California: 30, 31; Gran Torino. Regie: Clint Eastwood, Darsteller (v. l. n. r.): Ahney Her, Clint Eastwood. Warner Bros Pictures 2009. 30; Gran Torino. Regie: Clint Eastwood, Darsteller (v. l. n. r.): Bee Vang, John Caroll Lynch, Clint Eastwood. Warner Bros Pictures 2009. 31; Gran Torino. Regie: Clint Eastwood, Darsteller (v. l. n. r.): Brooke Chia Thao, Choua Kue, Bee Vang, Clint Eastwood, Ahney Her. Warner Bros Pictures 2009. 31; Gran Torino. Regie: Clint Eastwood, Darsteller (v. l. n. r.): Christoper Carley, Clint Eastwood. Warner Bros Pictures 2009. 31; Gran Torino. Regie: Clint Eastwood, Darsteller (v. l. n. r.): Clint Eastwood, Bee Vang. Warner Bros Pictures 2009. 30; Gran Torino. Regie: Clint Eastwood, Darsteller, Darsteller: Clint Eastwood. Warner Bros Pictures 2009. 31; Gran Torino. Regie: Clint Eastwood, Darsteller: Bee Vang. Warner Bros Pictures 2009. 30, 31, 31; Gran Torino. Regie: Clint Eastwood, Darsteller: Sonny Vue, Bee Vang (Thao), Lee Mong Vang, Jerry Lee, Elvis Thao. Warner Bros Pictures 2009. 30; Gran Torino. Regie: Clint Eastwood, Darstellerin: Dreama Walker. Warner Bros Pictures 2009. 30.